THE LECTURE METHOD
OF INSTRUCTION

The Instructional Design Library

Volume 27

THE LECTURE METHOD
OF INSTRUCTION

Martin M. Broadwell

Resources for Education and Management, Inc.
Decatur, Georgia

Danny G. Langdon

Series Editor

Educational Technology Publications
Englewood Cliffs, New Jersey 07632

Library of Congress Cataloging in Publication Data

Broadwell, Martin M
     The lecture method of instruction.

     (The Instructional design library; v. 27)
     Bibliography: p.
     1. Lecture method in teaching. I. Title.
II. Series: Instructional design library; v. 27.
LB2393.B76   371.39'6   79-23528
ISBN 0-87778-147-8

Printed in the United States of America.

Library of Congress Catalog Card Number:
79-23528.

International Standard Book Number:
0-87778-147-8.

First Printing: March, 1980.

FOREWORD

To ask someone to write on the lecture method was not easy. For someone to accept the assignment was pure bravery. To capture all that should be said is impossible. And, to anticipate that you, the reader, will agree with everything written here is not expected. The lecture method has been around for so many years and used by so many persons that we can't expect to capture the full measure of its use and design. Having said all this, Martin M. Broadwell is to be congratulated on having done a fine job. Both experienced teachers and novices will learn from this book.

Of course, lecturing is not *a* method. It is really a *combination* of methods, or at least it should be when one realizes the varied needs that usually must be met in the typical classroom. A wide range of such methods is described in this book.

Even though lecturing does encompass various methods, there are some design components that are common to all lecturing. Just to mention a few, we can all recognize the value of objectives, lesson plans and guides, interaction, and appropriate testing. When methods and components are tied to considerations related to environmental factors (room, lighting, visibility, etc.) and student factors (types, level, prerequisites, attitudes, etc.), then we can begin to build a lecture method—a design. Again, the author has captured these within the limited space afforded him in this publication.

In conclusion, the author realized, as I did, the risk involved in describing this design. But seeing that it is perhaps the most commonly used design in the classroom today, it was well worth the effort. Used, perhaps, as a measure of what we are currently doing in the way of lecturing and how it can be improved (for it *can* always be improved), or as a guide to the novice, we feel confident that what has been put into print is worthy of your attention.

Danny G. Langdon
Series Editor

PREFACE

To begin a book on the Lecture Method of Instruction takes a lot of nerve. Historically, lecturing has been maligned as a not-very-honorable profession. Then there is the question, "What is there to say about the lecture that would fill a book?" With both of these thoughts haunting me, I undertook to write this book, saving the "Preface" till last. Looking over the product, and even understanding my own writing limitations, I find the results, in all modesty, worthy of the reader's attention. This isn't immodesty. It is a revelation even to me that *there is something to making a good lecture*, as opposed to a mediocre one. There are some things we can do to make the prospects better, and it is a viable way to teach certain things and certain people.

As we have said, the lecture hasn't been too highly thought of over the years, especially in these days of all kinds of instructional technology and educational advances. But, look around us! Even today, what is the most prominent method being used in almost every institution where teaching is done in a collective way? Obviously, the lecture! For this reason, if for no other, it behooves us to not just write it off as something to be discussed only by the scullery maids. By following the steps laid down in this little collection of words, we can be better at it, and *much better* if we try just a little bit harder.

It would be foolish to pretend that all the things in this book came from this author. Even if there hadn't been any research, there have been years of experience in being a party to lecturing, both as the lecturer and the lecturee. To all those from whom I learned the many things I needed, I say *thanks*, and *thanks again*! There isn't a page in this book that doesn't result from looking back and thinking about some of my experiences under your guidance. Not all the experiences were that good, but from each I learned something.

In closing, I should especially like to thank Patricia O'Hara Langdon for her editorial assistance. Also, a special thanks to Denise Shillingford and Helen Levenstein for manuscript typing. It is nice to see how others can take my editorial and typing limitations and make me look so good.

M. M. B.

CONTENTS

ABSTRACT

THE LECTURE METHOD OF INSTRUCTION

The Lecture Method of Instruction is the single most commonly used teaching method in the world and by far the oldest existing method—and one of the least effective, if improperly used. It is an efficient means of communicating large amounts of information to many people in a short period of time. It allows the instructor to prepare ahead of time specific and logical data, with all the necessary lecture aids, thus making the end product a smooth presentation which can be offered several times over. Preparation, though easy, still needs care, when compared to other instructional designs. With the addition of visual aids, models, or group interaction, the lecture is enhanced to produce even more learning.

There are seven essential steps in the use of the lecture method of instruction. They include, in order: Student Analysis, Lesson Planning, Formation of the Lesson Guide, Preparation for Presenting the Lecture, Presentation of the Lecture, Testing, and Follow-up. The presentation of the lecture is the most visible part of the teaching method, of course, but lesson planning is the key to successful instruction. This has to include setting specific objectives for the students, proper use of time, collecting various teaching aids and supporting data, and a means of measuring how well the students have met the objectives. The versatility of the lecture method is such that it is virtually limitless in application, either to situation, subject matter, or student age and learning ability. There are many hazards in its use, but by using the design format, as described later, one can avoid most of the pitfalls and allow significant learning to take place.

THE LECTURE METHOD
OF INSTRUCTION

I.

USE

Essentially, the lecture has been used down through the years as a means of transmitting cognitive/factual data from a teacher to a group of students. It presupposes that the teacher is the expert, with all the data of access at the teacher's disposal rather than the students', and that the students need or want a large amount of this data in a short time. Basically, it is an efficient way of imparting information in a scheduled way without interruption, and with less planning than in most other teaching methods. However, from a learning-theory standpoint, it is a very low form of instruction as far as amount of knowledge retention is concerned.

Secondly, the lecture is used to effect desired changes either through cognitive reasoning or appealing to the affective domain to make changes through emotion. Usually, the lecture in the teaching-learning process is not used for emotional purposes. Nevertheless, it can and does change people's thinking through reasoning, as long as the lecturer follows certain rules of presenting logic. We can change people's thinking through the lecture, provided that they are accustomed to following reasoning without being involved in the process. As we will see later, it is possible to involve the learners in the lecture method with variations; and when this happens, the results are quite effective.

Best Uses

There are several *student* requirements for the lecture method to work well. Not everyone is able to follow a lecture, especially where a long period of concentration is required. If the lecturer is not very graphic in his or her presentation, or has some speech problems, the students who aren't trained to follow the lecture may get lost very quickly. On the other hand, when the learners are experienced in listening, they can follow the lecture easily enough and do well at it, even when the lecturer has shortcomings. Part of the requirement, then, is that the learners be experienced in learning from the lecture method. If the learners are technically oriented, for example, and have spent much time in listening to technical speakers, they generally do better in their retention (learning) than those without such opportunities. Further, the student who is able to listen and take notes is more likely to get the most value out of a lecture than those who find it difficult to listen and take notes at the same time. (Later on, we will direct our attention to the learner and see how note-taking can be improved.)

Another student requirement is that the students have had relatively successful learning experiences. We find that when students are successful at learning, they have a reduced amount of stress toward *any* method of teaching. Those who have not been successful at learning find the lecture method extremely threatening most of the time. This doesn't infer that only "smart" people can learn from the lecture. We are saying that those students who have had a successful history of learning experiences derived from different methods find it easier to learn from the lecture. We also find that people can "grow up to the lecture" with proper training and experiences. One thing that helps is the presence of positive reinforcement from a lecture through success at learning. For example, if a person who hasn't had much success at learning makes a good score on a test where most or all of the information came from a lecture, this reinforcement is a tremendous boost. The more successes that are present, the less likely it is that stress will be manifested, hence there will be less anxiety and probably more success at learning. So, one of the best uses of the lecture is for those students who have had success at learning and are able to handle verbal information in the oral format.

Another use that proves successful is where there is ready access by the learner of the same information as in the lecture. When the information is available in written or recorded form, the learner can use this for both clarification and review. This is especially helpful if the information is to be retained over a long period of time and the students don't have the ability to retain it without refreshing themselves on the various points made. By going to the information storage location, i.e., library, tape deck, video-cassette, etc., the student can get all or portions of the information again as needed. It isn't likely that the written or visual storage will be in exactly the same form as the lecture, so not only is there reinforcement but there is also an added advantage in that the information is presented in a sufficiently different way to provide more reinforcement for learning.

One final use of the lecture that is likely to produce above-average results is where the lecture can be supplemented or coordinated with visuals at the time of the presentation of the information. Not only will the visuals offer the same information in a different way, but will also cause the learner to use another sense to get the information. This almost always causes more learning/retention. If the lecturer is able to make a point in the lecture, then reinforce it with a graphic presentation of some sort, the learner has two senses operating and two chances of getting and understanding the information. It is an old illustration but it is still valid to demonstrate what we have just said by imagining the task of describing an elephant to a person without a picture, then realizing how much quicker, easier, and how many fewer words would be required if just one picture could be shown. More than that, we don't have to use much imagination to believe that the end learning result would be much better with the picture than it might be with the many words we would have had to use otherwise!

Poor Uses

Let's notice that there are some *poor* uses of the lecture, too. Unfortunately, poor uses of the lecture are frequently employed by even the most experienced of teachers. For instance, the lecture should not be used to present information to people with a history of short concentration spans. If people have an attention span of only a few minutes, and we provide them with a learning opportunity by lecturing for several hours with little or no break, then we and the students won't be too happy with the results of the learning experience. Those who are not used to long concentration spans cannot hold their attention for very long, even if they are very interested in getting the information. If they aren't involved in some kind of activity, if they are expected to listen to each word and take notes, and if they are required to do this over a sustained period of time, then the likelihood of the students losing their attention span is greatly increased. This is especially true until the students have had at least some practice at listening and note-taking activity. They are neither illiterate nor disinterested; they simply don't have the necessary skills to meet this kind of learning activity satisfactorily.

A second place where the lecture method is a poor choice for trying to get students to learn is where the students are resentful of the "teacher-dominant" role. People who strive to protect their independence dislike it when they see the teacher dominating the classroom. They feel that their independence is being threatened. This would be especially true where people are in a class with more intelligent students who are able to learn more quickly, after coming from a situation where they were "stars" in the class. It would be the same if they had come from a work environment where they had the lead roles, such as union stewardships, and found themselves having to retain and respond with current answers, and they couldn't bluff their way through in any satisfactory way.

A final ineffective use of the lecture method occurs when learners are forced to spend much of the time being inactive. On a normal day, they may be walking around, sitting for only brief periods, then going on the move again. With this as a background, they find sitting in a class a rather uncomfortable activity. If they happen to be involved in doing something in the classroom, then it is easier for them to concentrate on the subject being taught. But, to simply sit, listen, and *try to learn something* from a lecturer for more than a few minutes is almost impossible. This is compounded when the lecturer, who is accustomed to this arrangement, can't be empathetic to the learners. The lecturer tends to start blaming the students, saying that they aren't interested, or they lack motivation, or they should be disciplined in some way, etc. It is an uncomfortable situation for both the lecturer and the students. It is not an effective or efficient learning situation.

Variations in Usage

At a later point in this book, we will describe in detail some variations in using the lecture, combining it with other methods to get a better result. Rather than discuss that at this point, let's look at some variations in using the lecture in its "pure" form.

One such use is the "canned" lecture, where the presentation has been captured on videotape or film. In these cases, the students watching the video or film see exactly the same thing seen live by others at the original presentation. Depending upon the equipment used in the taping or filming, they may see slight variations in that there may be some close-ups or medium shots which take out some of the background, or provide close-ups of the chalkboard or other visuals. This is different from the original and may or may not be an improvement. In many cases, the replay is better than the original because it allows the viewer to focus directly on the speaker and provides none of the distractions common to the classroom environment. Added to this is the use of media which appeal to many in today's society (movies and television) and which are an effective use of the lecture. On the other hand, if a lecture is dull, long, or ineffective in its original form, video and film can do very little to improve it. The end result is almost always *worse* than the original.

Another slight variation on the lecture which is popular in some circles is the use of audio-cassette recordings. The lecture is taped, perhaps live, and then made available to other students who were not present during the original presentation. For those who missed the first effort, and who want or need the information, this is an easy and inexpensive way to get the spoken word. It lacks something, obviously, but the *information* is there (assuming it is a good recording) and the student can listen at his or her leisure. Some obvious problems arise. First, visuals, chalkboard work, etc., can't be reproduced on the cassette. If questions arise about the material, it is too late to ask them when listening to the cassette. (The same is true of video and film.) The only thing that can be helpful is listening to the other questions that were asked and the answers given.

Audio recording is used also by students at the original lecture, who record the lecture and expect to use the material as a review or to study in more detail, *but don't do it*. The problem is that the students may fully expect to listen again in the quiet of their study environment. As a result, they tend to rely on the recording too heavily, *instead of paying attention during the original lecture*. Or, they tend to find security in knowing they can listen again and again if necessary, so they fail to ask questions. This puts a heavy dependence on the cassette tape and, if they don't listen to it in undisturbed concentration, their learning is reduced drastically. Unfortunately, the two situations may end up being counter-productive. They don't listen too well in class, thinking that they will listen more closely to the tape; and then they don't listen to the tape, thinking that they have already heard enough to get the information. The end result is lack of sufficient learning to justify the time put into the lecture in the first place. Lectures require student attention—every bit as much as teacher-lecturer attention.

II.

OPERATIONAL DESCRIPTION

Of all the teaching techniques known in educational circles —at any level of instruction—the lecture is by far the most familiar and most often used. We will deal with a number of variations of the lecture and different ways of using it, but in its simplest form the lecture is merely *telling somebody something*. Historically, it dates as far back as history is recorded. There is a good reason for its longevity. Before printing was easy and cheap, only a few had access to knowledge through books (if books existed at all), so individuals passed their information on to others through the lecture method, which was the easiest means available. We find teachers, scientists, and scholars throughout history resorting to this simple process, though we find them using variations, as will be discussed in this chapter. The lecture is not always just a one-way process with no involvement or action from the students. Good lecturers can get much involvement and feedback from the students. The lecture is, for them, only a means to an end, not an end in itself.

Straight Lecture
As we saw in our simple definition above, there is a form of the lecture that doesn't require any activity on the part of the student. The "straight" lecture is the simplest form—that is, the teacher presents the material, with the goal being that

11

the students will absorb the information presented. In this form, there is a large burden placed on the instructor, since everything that happens comes from the front of the room. The instructor prepares notes from whatever research is done, brings the notes to the class, and chooses the best words he or she can think of to transmit the message. The words may be thought of ahead of time, and there may be practice, but when classtime comes, the teacher is in control. The system of instructing in the straight lecture not only puts the instructor in control, in front of the room, but also *requires* that control. Usually, the students are facing the front in a "traditional" arrangement of rows and perhaps columns. Sometimes audio-visual or other types of equipment are available to be projected or used at the front of the room. The teacher's concerns are: to be heard, to be understood, to allow for students to see visuals, to be able to see the students, and to cover a prespecified amount of material in the time allotted. There is no questioning of the students orally during the presentation, though there may be some type of written quiz interspersed with the lecture, or a test may be given at the end of certain units. There is no effort made to get feedback from the students in the form of involvement or oral discussion. Evaluation of the teaching is usually done by observing the results of student quizzes or examinations.

The lecture does not necessarily cover only new material. The students may have been given preclass assignments in the form of problems or outside reading. There may be individual or sub-group work done outside of class or at other periods during the course time. The students may have even been involved in some form of research, reading, or investigation, but at the time they come to the lecture, the teacher—in the straight lecture mode—provides all input. Discussion on the reading, outside work, or research is either done at another time or is covered by the instructor in his or her lecture.

Chalk-talk Lecture

Over the years, instructors have used what is commonly referred to as the "chalk-talk," which is just exactly that. The instructor, with chalk in hand, lectures and illustrates the lecture with chalk on the chalkboard. In recent years, there have been variations of this, with the advent of flip-chart easels, overhead transparency projectors, and other means of writing and lecturing at the same time. The idea, of course, is to enhance the words with pictures or additional words, drawn or written during the presentation. This is intended to reinforce the spoken word and add to the likelihood that the words will be remembered, since an additional sense is stimulated. Usually, the instructor has planned to present the material in such a way that a certain drawn or written concept will offer additional enlightenment for the students. The "board work" may even be contained in the notes of the instructor.

Even here, there is room for variation. The instructor may spend the first part of the lecture just talking, with no use of chalk or marking pens. When it is obvious that the students are ready for a change of pace, the instructor moves to the writing surface in an effort to regain interest or rekindle enthusiasm. This can be a spontaneous thing or planned from previous experience. (Some instructors are able to "sense" when it is time for this change of pace; others build it in.) Using the chalkboard suggests that the writing, or the point made with the writing, is temporary and that the information can be erased. If the flip-chart easel is used, the material may be reused at a later time and the instructor may mark where the material can be found with a tab of some kind. If there is a question from the class or a need to refresh the group, the instructor can simply go to the easel pad and flip back to the page or pages required. Sometimes, the material put on the easel is deemed so important that the instructor may tear off the sheet and place it on the wall with some form of tape or adhesive.

When using the overhead projector with a lecture, the instructor uses marking pens on an acetate sheet that is transparent. The instructor can write and still *face the students*, which is sometimes an improvement over the chalkboard or even the flip-chart easel. There are several ways the pens and acetate may be used. The simplest is to use a blank acetate, which may be clear or tinted almost any color and written upon much as one would on the chalkboard or easel. The difference, of course, is that once anything is written on the acetate, it can be saved (by saving the acetate) and used any time later. Some prefer to use "permanent" pens, others like the water-based pens which can be erased simply with a wet cloth. There are solutions which erase the permanent marks, but water will not affect it.

Another use of the pens and acetate is to have some portion of the marking already on the acetate—maybe the lines of a form to be filled out—in permanent ink. During instruction, the form can be filled out, even erased by using the water-based pens, and still retain a reusable record for later reference. There are many processes for transferring pictures or type onto the acetates ahead of time. One thing to bear in mind about the use of acetates and marking pens is that acetates are inexpensive. They can be erased completely, even when the "permanent" markers are used, and are reusable many times. Most kinds, though, will begin to show age after many uses, and even those that have been prepared and transferred ahead of time finally will have to be redone.

Guided Note-taking Lecture

One of the many variations of the lecture that allows for some student participation, though not orally, is the process of preparing student note-taking devices ahead of the lecture.

In their most complex form, the entire lecture is programmed out to such an extent that the students can follow along with almost every word the lecturer says, though the lecture itself is not written out. Rather, the notes are prepared in such a way that the students have blanks to fill in, questions to answer, outlines to complete, and conclusions to reach. There may even be references for further study or referral by the students. Obviously, while this is of much help to the students, it is time-consuming and restrictive for the instructor. A simpler form of this mode is more practical and accomplishes many of the same advantages. There is a general outline provided, where enough information is presented that the students can tell at any time what points are being made, but they have to make most of the notes themselves. There may simply be some questions over the material, in the order in which it is presented, and the students answer with brief statements or conclusions as they hear the material given from the instructor. Ideally, whichever method is used, the students will be able to draw their own conclusions. Insofar as retention from a lecture is concerned, nothing is more effective than having the students think through the material presented to the point where they actually get to draw their own conclusions on the subject being taught.

Slide Lecture

There will be no effort to discuss in this book the preparation and use of the many kinds of visual aids that are available to the instructor, but we will deal with the use of visuals in connection with the lecture.

This method, sometimes called the illustrated lecture or slide-talk, involves presenting visuals along with a lecture in order to make the points clearer with the use of graphics of some type. We have already touched on the use of the overhead transparency. There is also the opaque projector, which allows the lecturer to show illustrations direct from a photograph or any kind of printed or illustrated original, without having to reproduce or harm the original in any way. This allows the teacher to bring reference books or graphics to class, show the pictures in full color, make whatever points need to be made, and then replace the original for future use and reference. This has a disadvantage in that it usually precludes any duplication for the students to have as reference themselves, which is an advantage of the overhead transparency projection.

Many instructors like the use of slides to accompany their lecture. When they have access to the reproduction facilities that prepare slides, this is effective and reasonably inexpensive, if used several times to teach the same materials. The slides, which can be in color with little added expense and effort, are usually mounted on cardboard or plastic mounts and identified with a number, name, or code. They are then placed in some kind of slide holder that will fit a projector that is advanced with an impulse generated by pushing a button. The instructor usually has access to this by means of a long cord. Most units allow for focus, advance, back-up, and on and off at the same control switch. This may be mounted on a speaker's stand or hand-held by the teacher. The teacher will have the notes prepared on the lecture in such a way that the slides are keyed to the lecture. As the teacher is ready for the next slide, he or she simply pushes the "advance" button. If there will be a period of nonuse, the projector is either turned off or an opaque slide is inserted so that the screen will not have anything projected upon it. Copies of these slides can be reproduced from the original artwork and placed in the students' notebooks or for handout purposes.

What has been said above applies to still-projected pictures, whether in slide, transparency, or continuous slide-film (or filmstrip) format. There are occasions when the instructor will do the same thing with a moving picture, without sound, and offer narration along the way. This is effective, since motion is much more attention-catching than is the still slide. The obvious drawback to this is cost and difficulty of preparation. Most teachers have neither the budget nor the facilities for preparing movies. Some take existing movies and turn off the sound, preferring to furnish their own narration at intervals along the way. This, too, is effective and is even a good way to make an old film last a little longer, if the narration is the only thing that is outmoded. The instructor can change the words or even point out where visual changes have occurred in the updating process of the subject being discussed.

Lecture Demonstration

There are times when the instructor wants to present information about a piece of equipment or an experiment of some kind, or show specific procedures. The most common way of doing this, in the absence of a good series of visuals, is to bring the actual machine or experiment into the classroom and give a lecture demonstration on the subject. If the students are in a position to see well enough, this is an excellent way to get the points across—even better than a film, if visibility is no problem. A model, resembling the object under consideration or the actual object itself, is then brought into the class and made to operate just as it might in the "real world." The instructor checks it out ahead of time, builds this portion of the lecture around the unit, and then, when the class begins, proceeds to describe the unit or equipment and gives whatever background is necessary to understand it. Assuming there is no "hands-on" activity, that is, the students are not working or experimenting on the equipment, the teacher must depend upon his or her prowess at operating the equipment as well as being able to discuss and demonstrate it so that the students can hear, see, and understand.

The lecture demonstration has many advantages in the teaching-learning process, mainly because it adds the fascination of a piece of real-life equipment and some action to the classroom. It represents a change of pace and almost always increases student interest. The actual equipment is better than any description of it and usually better than pictures of it. It helps "program" the instructor's lecture, too, making it easy for the words and description to flow, since the equipment usually needs to operate in a sequence of some kind. The words have much more meaning, being reinforced with an actual happening or action by the equipment. One caution for the instructor is to get the equipment to work, rather than just pointing out to the students that "if we had time, we could see it do thus and so ..." Also, have the students look at it ahead of time so they will be somewhat familiar with what is being discussed during the lecture.

Lecture-Discussion

A final classification of the lecture is the lecture-discussion. This is where the instructor presents material that is new to the students, in lecture form, then engages in a discussion about the material. It is usually the most effective of the modes discussed so far because it involves the students in thought-and-response kinds of ways. It serves to get feedback on student thinking and helps them get feedback for their own evaluation of their learning. The instructor may use any one of the methods suggested so far in getting the material to the students in the first place, whether straight lecture, guided note-taking, or even the lecture demonstration. This comes from the notes prepared ahead of class time by the instructor. Since there is no way the instructor can prepare the students' questions and comments, only the *time* can be built in. The instructor outlines the presentation in such a way that there is time allotted for student participation. Even the students' guides may include some mention of discussion. The instructor's guide certainly does, though it may leave some leeway for exactly when this takes place.

Effective teachers often anticipate the classes' questions or comments ahead of time, and prepare for them with back-up data or references. They may even jot down prospective questions and some memory "joggers" to remind them of comments they want to make to the students if such questions are asked. If the same material is taught repeatedly, the instructor will know what to expect most of the time. The instructor may program the discussion even further by preparing "discussion questions" to be asked along the way to begin the discussion. This allows for much more control, since the instruction can go along smoothly until the teacher is ready for some discussion. The discussion is on specific things, too, and this makes preparation much easier.

Specifically, the lecture-discussion process goes like this. There is input from the instructor, presented in such a way as to lead the students' thinking in certain ways. At certain predetermined or spontaneous points, the students become involved in one of the ways just mentioned. The purpose is to get them involved, to allow them to advance their thinking further along, to get feedback for the instructor, and to allow the students to get feedback for themselves. Let's look at some of the ways this discussion begins and progresses.

First, there is the simple question-and-answer method. The teacher asks a question and the students answer. The students may be called on by name, they may be allowed to volunteer, or they may even get together in small groups to consider the answer. The instructor can handle the right and wrong answers in different ways, to be discussed in detail later. When the answer comes, the teacher may accept it, reflect it back to the rest of the class for more discussion, or modify it and go on to the next point. Each kind of reaction has its own advantage and disadvantage. Each has the advantage of getting the involvement and feedback mentioned earlier.

Another way that questions and answers may play a part in the lecture-discussion mode of instructing is where the students ask the question and the teacher handles the answer. This may come from the instructor simply asking, "Are there any questions?" Many times this is all that is needed to get a discussion going. Here, again, there are several ways of handling these questions, either by answering them or reflecting them in various ways back to the group. One question can be used to generate discussion or to generate additional questions. One question may be answered with another and the discussion kept going in this manner. The students can also get into the questioning as a result of the teacher asking "leading" questions or making suggestions that cause the students to begin to have doubts about their understanding of a certain subject. This usually will lead to one of them asking a question for clarification. Often, there will be a chorus of "Yeah, what about that?" from other perplexed students. Even without the question, the teacher can lead to this perplexing point and ask a question of one or more of the students to get things going.

Some instructors prefer to build questions into the student handouts. The questions are a part of the lecture notes. They may be intended to expand on a particular subject. In this case, the question is built on information that has already been presented but it asks the students to carry the topic forward some more, with additional input from their past knowledge or experience. This allows the subject to be broadened with student input. The instructor may add some information—he or she may "prod" the students to remember something which was said earlier or may just wait it out.

Whatever happens, it usually proves to be interesting for the instructor as well, allowing for some good feedback on how well the subject is understood up to this point.

Other instructors prefer to use the question-and-answer time to simply stop and see where the students are "right now." The questions are a review of what has been said, and successful answers mean successful teaching. It is a form of "final exam," though the questions may be oral and answered by only a few of the students. If there is a good random sample, it is reliable information. If only one student answers all the questions, the information is virtually useless as a test of how well the whole class has done.

Then, there is the "mind-stretching" use of questions and answers. This is a case where the teacher lays a foundation of facts and even conclusions. With this well-established, and even with some kind of testing to assure that the information has been properly received, the teacher poses some question that is apparently far-removed from the subject at hand or that is obviously not a direct question over the material just covered. It is obvious, too, that some thought will have to be put into finding the answer. The question is not one that can be answered from past knowledge or experience. It is a question that must take some of these things into consideration, but it requires in-depth thought before finding a proper answer. It is truly a "thought question." While some students can't handle such assignments and others fail to see any value in them, most will enjoy the mental gymnastics. It isn't something that should be carried on for great lengths, even if the students enjoy it, since it fails to add much *new* data. After a while, the enjoyment may overshadow the learning, though this isn't much of a hazard in most cases. It is a good teaching technique, and, when used properly, will get the students working their minds even during the regular lecture portions of the instructing.

Summary

Summarizing what has been said so far, we have seen that there are different modes of the lecture, with variations in the modes themselves. The simplest form is the *straight lecture*, where the instructor does all the talking, based on prepared notes, and the students listen, take notes, and get their learning in whatever way they choose. There is no student involvement in this mode.

Next, there is the *chalk-talk* approach to lecturing. In this case, the instructor not only presents the information in oral form, but also uses some device, such as the chalkboard or overhead transparency, to help make the points. The use of the pen or chalk adds the possibility of more words, drawings, or a combination of each.

There is the *guided note-taking* process where the lecturer prepares a set of notes or questions for the students that follow in the same sequence as the lecture and allows the students to listen with more direction than without the guided notes. The guided notes can vary from a briefly-worded outline to a many-worded set of notes with places for answers, notes, and even the opportunity to fill in blanks and draw conclusions.

The *slide lecture* makes use of visual aids, with color or black and white slides, with preproduced transparencies or opaque drawings, or with 35mm filmstrips, or even with a silent movie that is narrated by the instructor.

If there is equipment to be taught about or procedures that require demonstrating, there is the *lecture demonstration*. This adds a touch of realism to the class and allows the students to see the actual equipment or a model of it in operation. The instructor lectures and demonstrates at the same time, letting the students see as well as hear the procedures.

Finally, there is the *lecture-discussion* method of instructing. This is where the students get involved, either by asking questions of the teacher or in answering questions from the teacher. This method has the advantage of giving the teacher and the students a chance to get feedback.

III.

DESIGN FORMAT

The lecture as a method is not complete without the obvious elements of students, teachers, and places to lecture. Before we can fully understand the aspects of the lecture design, we have to examine the background activities and planning that must go into a successful lecture. For the most part, this must be done by the teacher. Some of it can be done by others and some of the information can come *through* others, but the main responsibility still lies with the lecturer. It is not a vain cliché that says nothing is ever *done well* that isn't *planned well*. As we look into the design formatting of the lecture, we have to look first at the planning that leads up to successful lectures. We will look also at the various types and modes of lectures and see what makes up their design, after looking at the course planning that is necessary before undertaking the lecture. We will look at the following in the order shown (and as further detailed in Figure 1).

- Student Analysis
- Lesson Planning
- Formation of the Lesson Guide
- Preparation for Presenting the Lecture
- Presentation of the Lecture
- Testing
- Follow-up

Student Analysis

It is not enough to determine *what* we are going to teach; we must put equal vigor into deciding *whom* we will be teaching. Even if we have no control over the students and no veto over their being in our class, we still need to know a number of things about them. Admittedly, we will not be able to find out everything about every student, but with a little effort, we can get a relatively good profile of the *typical* student or the characteristics of the bulk of our student population. We can also find out the extremes of the students with the same effort. Here are some things we will need to know before we face them in our lecture:

(1) their general age and age distribution;
(2) their previous learning experiences;
(3) prerequisite learning levels;
(4) general acceptance of the teaching-learning environment;
(5) their reasons for taking this particular course; and
(6) their likelihood of success, based on experience of other teachers.

Since it isn't our aim to deal with the student end of the teaching-learning situation, we will not go into detail on the above, other than to say that if we don't find out some of the things in enough detail to be meaningful, we are missing an opportunity to be much more successful than we would otherwise be in lecturing. An expanded discussion of the above list is found in the Developmental Guide chapter.

Lesson Planning

The successful lecture has been *planned* successfully. Many things have come together to make up this plan, and much thought has been put into the content. We will deal here with the typical elements making up the good lesson plan. Again, since we are primarily concerned with the lecture itself, we

Figure 1

DESIGN FORMAT *for Lecture*

I. **Student Analysis**

II. **Lesson Planning**
   A. Name of Lecture
   B. Objectives
   C. Timing
      1. Change of Pace
      2. Time of Day
   D. Teaching Aids
   E. References/Supporting Data
   F. Outline
   G. Summary
   H. Testing

III. **Formation of the Lesson Guide**

IV. **Preparation for Presenting the Lecture**
   A. Stage Fright
   B. Preparing the Room

V. **Presentation of the Lecture**
   A. Introduction
   B. Main Body—Substantive
   C. Main Body—Applications/Examples
   D. Summary/Conclusion

VI. **Testing**

VII. **Follow-up**

---

will not have space to exhaust the subject completely. Enough information will be given so that the reader can prepare a lesson plan. Generally, the lesson plan should include the following items and for the most part be prepared in the order given.

A. *Name of Lecture*

It may seem insignificant to some, but giving the lecture a title is one sure way to narrow the lecture itself down to more specific things. When we name the lecture, we have said, "This is what we are going to talk the *most* about." If we find that it is a struggle to give our lecture a title, it may be that we haven't yet decided on the *exact area of concentration*. We may need to spend less time on trying to figure out a title and more time weeding out some of the generalities of the planned lecture. The title should be as precise as possible—*and specific*. The title is part of the promise we are making to the students, and we want the promise to be as believable and realistic as possible. If we promise them something nebulous in the title, something that allows us to go off in almost any direction, then that is probably what will happen. The students will never know exactly what we were going to talk about, and won't know exactly what we *did* talk about. If we can be precise and meaningful in the title, they will know where they are going and we will be more likely to take them there.

B. *Objectives*

There should be an overall course objective that becomes a contract between the students and the instructor. At the end of the course, the successful students *will be able to do certain things*. We prepare these contracts, these goals, these objectives before we prepare the lectures that will get them there. We don't stop there, though. Not only do we do this for the overall course, but also for the individual lectures. We figure out the subject, give it a specific title, then ask ourselves, "Okay, what do I expect the students to be able to do when the lecture is over that they can't do now?" We can tell by these objectives just what direction the lecture should take. We can tell how difficult the content is going to be to teach by what we expect the students to be able to do. These objectives should be measurable, too. If the objectives are vague, then the lecture will be, too. If we say something like, "The students will be able to understand the significance of events surrounding the happenings beginning ...," we can go anywhere with the lecture, and they may end up *anywhere*, also. If we say something like, "Will be able to identify and show the causes that brought about the events that resulted in . . .," then we are much more specific, and both we and the students know what it is we are going to be talking about.

As for levels of teaching and learning difficulty, the objectives will tell us that, too. At the lowest level, we are simply asking the students to memorize certain things. Our objectives in this case will read like, "The students will be able to list (or name, or quote) ..." Since this lowest level of difficulty is mostly memory work, we usually classify it at the "knowledge" level, in which we ask the students to be able to "quote" something. It takes little thought to reach the objective. *It doesn't even take an understanding of the subject matter*. We usually classify "understanding" or comprehension of the subject matter in a next higher level of difficulty. Since understanding requires some study and thought, it is more difficult to teach and to learn. We can tell them when we are asking the students to reach this level. We now say that if they are successful, "they will be able to explain (or describe, or put into their own words) ..." Since the only way we will ever know if they really comprehend something is to hear them *explain it in their own words*, we use this as the way to tell if we are striving for this level of learning. When we write our objectives in such a way as to expect the students to go beyond the memory level (quoting), and actually show some comprehension, we use some form of "putting it into their own words" in the objectives.

The next level is even harder to teach and to learn. There are times when we want them to do more than just quote or even put something in their own words. We want them to understand it to the point that they can actually make an application (or see application) for what we have been talking about. We call this the "application" level, and measure it in application terms. We aren't talking about being able to go out and do some application, necessarily. As far as the lecture is concerned in relation to the student's thinking process, it would be sufficient for the student to be able to recognize or give an example of that which we have lectured about. The objective would be written in this frame of reference: "The student will be able to distinguish between ..." or "Given a set of alternatives, the student will be able to recognize the one that fits the criteria we have set down ..."

So, as we plan our lecture and plan the objective for it, we think in terms of the levels of learning, as shown below:

| APPLICATION: "Be able to give or recognize an example." |
| COMPREHEND: "Be able to put into own words." |
| KNOWLEDGE: "Be able to quote." |

Levels of difficulty of
teaching and learning.

C. *Timing*

After we have gotten our objectives well-established and

defined in measurable terms, and we have decided that the title of the lecture and the objectives match, we start thinking in terms of *timing*. Timing is more than just deciding how long the lecture is going to be, or even how we are going to allot our time to various topics within the lecture, although it certainly includes these considerations. We have made a commitment to the students in the objectives, so we can't just forget about timing and lecture until time runs out. We need to allocate enough time for each of the topics and each of the objectives in such a way that the students will be able to follow the material we are dealing with, take notes, and do whatever assignments we might have built into the lecture. But timing goes beyond that. We have to consider the students' attention span. We have to realize that the less they are involved, the shorter their attention span is. In the following, we will take up two related considerations to timing.

1. *Change of Pace.* There are some things we can do to *extend* the attention span during a lecture. We aren't talking about extending it by making the lecture more interesting or exciting, though that is certainly something we ought to try to do. No doubt that would help! Beyond this, however, there are some things we can do to make it possible for the students to concentrate on the lecture for a longer period of time. It isn't very difficult to do, and with almost no practice we can become proficient at it. All we have to do is use some of the "change of pace" techniques that are available to any instructor. By change of pace, we refer to doing something different enough that the students' interest will be increased *just by the change itself.*

Let's see some of the ways this can be accomplished. If we have a great deal of material to cover and we think that a lecture is the best way, but feel that it will be difficult for the students to concentrate for the length of time needed to complete the lecturing, we should do all we can to make the lecture interesting. We can go for as long as we think the students can follow without losing interest, then cut over to a chalk-talk. For instance, we move from behind the speaker's stand, go to the board, and begin to diagram some of the lecture. We do it deliberately, and with some enthusiasm. We make it such that the students will want to take nòtes. We may even suggest taking notes. We point out the value of understanding what is being put on the board. This doesn't have to be very long. Even if we go no more than eight to ten minutes, the audience is back with us, and we have made it possible to return to the straight lecture mode for perhaps another ten minutes and still hold their attention. We can't hold it as long as the first time, but we have successfully extended it for a reasonable period of time to make it worth the effort.

This process can be continued for an extended period of lecturing, then giving a change of pace, then lecturing some more. Using any one of the variations on the lecture discussed earlier, we can keep the students' interest up much longer than with just the straight lecture. We can get additional mileage out of some student involvement, such as the lecture-discussion mode, because the students are physically as well as mentally involved. When the discussion starts, they look around at the person talking, wait their turn by watching the other students, then look for nods of approval when they are talking. When it becomes obvious that the teacher expects them to participate and is giving them a chance to do so, they quickly get into mental involvement, too. They start to ask themselves if they really understand what is being said, if they know enough to contribute, if they have questions, etc. All of this builds their "concentration quotient" higher, so that the lecture that follows will hold their attention longer than it would have otherwise. The lecture-discussion need only last for a few minutes to build this quotient. In fact, the alert teacher will recognize that not only is the discussion intended to get feedback, but it also serves the purpose of building the concentration capability for the lecture to follow. Therefore, he or she limits the discussion period. Of course, if we decide that the discussion is important for getting the information across, then we don't cut it off just to get back to the lecture. We are talking about limiting the discussion when our reason for allowing it was to extend the concentration span of the students.

2. *Time of Day.* Another time consideration, which also has to do with the ability to concentrate, is the time of day the lecture is scheduled. There are times during the day when students are better able to listen for longer periods of time without losing their concentration. Of course, students differ, and therefore we can only speak in generalities on this subject, because there will always be exceptions—those who have longer concentration spans at different times. But there are some general rules that will apply to all situations.

It seems that people have to *warm up to listening*. This means that it is very difficult for them to come right into a class, the very first thing in the morning, and be good concentrators. If we start off the day with a long and unexciting lecture, not many of the students will follow attentively. This is not a situation where they have a *short* attention span, but rather a case of not having started listening yet. We can avoid this problem easily enough by doing something different at the beginning of the day, until students have "warmed up." We could give some kind of lecture demonstration, for example. We could use the lecture-discussion, which gets students thinking, talking, and active. Ten to 15 minutes of this will get them prepared to listen to a longer lecture. Another way to start students thinking early is to give them a *short quiz*. The quiz should be over material discussed previously, and it should require only short answers. This isn't the place for long, subjective answers that require extensive, deep concen-

tration. Since we know that many of the students haven't yet
started to function in a classroom setting this early in the
day, we should be careful as to how we use the results of
the quiz. We ought to consider that the quiz is being used as a
means of warming up the students for the listening to be
done later and not to get feedback on their recall of a previous learning experience.

If we have a series of interesting slides or a film that deals
with things we will be lecturing about next, this is a good
time to use such visuals. We usually find that prepared slides
or films get the students thinking about listening. The idea
isn't just to "wake them up" in the morning. It is simply to
spend a few minutes preparing them so that they can concentrate on the material that will be presented in a less than
optimal time period for most students. Determining how long
it will take us to get them ready for longer attention spans
depends upon how long they have been awake and how much
listening they have already done. Some students will already
have been studying and reading, and perhaps will even have
discussed some of the material with others. These will be
ready sooner, of course, but even here it is better that they
do something other than start the class listening to a lecture.
Remember, we are referring to a *short period of warm-up*,
not an hour or so.

The beginning of the day isn't the only time we have to
worry about. Obviously, the end of the day is going to be a
problem time to enable students to learn, to listen, and to
concentrate. If they have been listening to lectures all day,
they will have a hard time keeping their attention span up for
a long period of time at the end of the day. But here is a situation where we might *not* be successful if we resorted to a
film or series of slides. Boredom and mental fatigue may have
set in by now, and when the lights go out, so do the students'
minds! Unless there are some very exciting things on the

screen, and unless they have a large amount of accountability for the things being presented, students fail to give it all their attention. There are some things we can do at the end of the day to keep students with us during the lecture period.

One of the things that is good any time in the late afternoon or evening is to have some kind of lecture demonstration where students can see and even work with the equipment. If we scatter this through the session, intermixed with short periods of lecture, we will be more likely to keep them with us for longer periods. If we have them only for an hour, we follow the same pattern, since we have the same problem. We start off by *showing* them something they can touch, even if it is something they can pass around the room. Then we lecture for a short period—no more than 20 to 30 minutes —then change pace again. Perhaps we can build in some kind of thought question or challenge. If we take even three or four minutes to challenge them, we will find that they will "last" longer. Even breaking them into paired groups for one question will help. Ideally, it can be a challenge of "let's see which group can come up with the most ... or the first ... or the most unique ..." Putting students into sub-groups for even a minute or two is better than challenging them individually, because some individuals won't get involved to the point that their minds are temporarily free so that they are thus able to absorb more lecturing. In sub-groups, we find that most students will talk at least a little, and this is enough to extend their concentration a bit longer.

Around the middle of the day is also a problem. If we have the lecture time just before lunch, we are indeed in trouble, if we aren't careful to use good techniques. Right before lunch is a good time to do some testing. There is nothing wrong with students' concentration. It is their *interest* that may be lagging, because they are thinking about things they have to do at lunch break. If we begin the lecture with a note that they will have a short quiz toward the end of the period, over the material discussed in the lecture, we may be pretty sure that we will have their interest for most of the lecture time. This means to actually give a quiz—not a threat of one— which covers the material in the lecture. It, too, can be short, since we are only trying to keep students alert for the lecture. Announcing a quiz over the material is always a good way to interest students in the material, but this gets "old-hat" after a while and eventually will lose its effect.

Right after lunch is perhaps the worst period of the day to have a lecture. Coming into a stuffy room, sitting down, and listening to a monotoned lecture isn't the pattern we would give for an ideal learning situation, especially if the students have just finished a heavy, starchy lunch. But we have material to cover and we have goals to meet, and this is the time of day assigned for us to do it. "What can we do?" First, there are some things we *can't do* and expect learning to take place. We can't show a movie with the lights down low or out altogether. Most of the students will miss the opening bars of music in the film because *they will already be asleep*. It is also a bad time to give a quiz, for the same reasons. If there ever was an appropriate time for some physical activity, this is it! It is also the time for short lectures followed by discussions, sub-group activity, more lecture, more discussion, more lecture, more "chalk-talk," more demonstration, more lecture, and so on. Even in an hour, the time will be more meaningful if we can come up with as much change of pace as possible. It doesn't have to be an even balance. Just as long as we don't lecture too long without stopping, we are all right. Fifteen or 20 minutes at a time is probably the best we can do, but we can gain this time over and over again, if we break the lecture up for even five minutes of interaction within the group.

D. *Teaching Aids*

When we start to think about a lecture, even one we have given many times before, we should immediately start to ask ourselves, "What kind of materials will I need to do this lecture successfully?" "Materials" includes equipment, handouts, teaching aids, and anything that exists in addition to the lecture. We need to think of the lecture notes and see if they need updating. How about slides or overhead transparencies we plan to use? Are they together? Accurate? In order? Do we have enough copies of the handouts we plan to use? If we are planning to use guided notes, have we checked one last time to be certain that they match the lesson outline we will be using? Have we checked our "checklist" in our lesson plan and found that we have everything we need? (Do we even have a checklist?) Since we are talking about the lesson plan in this section, we need to remember that any good lesson plan includes a checklist to remind us that there are certain things to be done, to be gathered together, and to be printed up for the lecture. It goes with our notes and is used *every time* we go to give a lecture. If not, we will start lecturing from memory and discover after it is too late that our memory isn't as good as we thought it was!

The same is true for student materials, if we plan to have any. If there are things that are important for the students to have, like samples of pages or charts or graphs or tables or pieces of equipment, our lesson plan should include these, with a checklist as mentioned above for the teaching aids. We can't leave this up to somebody else to *check on*. We can let somebody else do it, but we need to make one final check; having reference to it in the lesson plan will make us remember it.

E. *References/Supporting Data*

A good lesson plan will include notations on all of the

references and other supporting data used in the lecture. It may not have copies of all the material, but where it is likely to be questioned, we should think seriously of having this in the lesson material along with our notes and other materials we have gathered. A check of all the sources we plan to refer to will give us a guide for gathering things together in the lesson plan. Some like to have a handout available with a bibliography of back-up data. While this is helpful, it isn't necessary for every lecture we give. The reference material we are talking about for the lesson plan is mainly for *our use* in case we have to check something. We may have to check something because a student asks a question, of course, but this is still primarily for our own use. There is much comfort in knowing that there is a back-up reference for the things we say that might be questioned. Also, it is comforting to know that we can always go back and refresh ourselves with the data, because we have included the reference in our lesson plan. Just where we put the information in the lesson plan is a matter of personal choice. Some like to have it in with the notes and copies of handouts in the order in which they are used. Others prefer to have the material, that is essentially reference or back-up, placed in an appendix and numbered in such a way that it is easy to locate but not in the way of the notes.

A note of caution with regard to reference material: Time has a way of flying when it comes to reference material. If we are referring to a study of some kind and that study is critical to our lecture points, we should make an effort to keep our files up-to-date on the study. If new studies have been made, we are in trouble if we don't know about them and the students then refer to them. About the worst thing we can do is to read about something in a journal or paper, not save it, then decide we should refer to it later in a lecture. When somebody wants more information on the subject—and they will—we feel helpless when we have to say, "Well, I'm sorry, but I can't put my hands on that right now." Even worse, it is a problem if we have won an argument with the data, then can't produce it!

F. *Outline*

It perhaps goes without saying that every lesson plan should have a good outline. The outline is the heart of any lecture. We may have notes, reference materials, handouts, guided notes for the students, and many visual aids, but the one thing that ties it all together is the outline. Regardless of how we make the outline, it is the one place we can go for the big picture, the overall view of what we plan to cover, what we plan for the order of the presentation, and roughly the amount of time allocated to each topic. For many, it becomes the lecture notes as well, especially if it is a lecture we give more than once. We need these other things, but the outline is essential to continuity.

How do we get the outline? Some prefer to start with objectives, and that is the best way to be sure that everything follows the topic and relates to the objectives. One of the most efficient ways of making an outline is the use of small index cards, 3x5 or 4x6 being about the right size. We place our objective on one card, preferably a different color from all the rest. This is the objective for just one key point, remember, so there will be several objectives, hence several cards of that color. Behind each of these cards will be the key points we want to make, not the supporting data and facts as yet. As we develop these stacks of cards behind the objective card, we lay them out on the table or desk and begin to find out some things. First, we may find that we don't have a very good distribution of cards. Some objectives have many cards behind them, while others have practically none. When this happens, we revisit the objectives and decide if we have put too much material into any one objective and are thus taking too big of a bite by having only one objective. We also look to see if we have stretched things out too far with several objectives where we can narrow them down to a lesser number.

Using the cards has another advantage, too. It is the easiest way to rearrange the lecture. All we do is move the cards from one place to another. We can also shift points from one objective to another, if we think certain things should be said earlier or later. It allows us to experiment with different orders and use some imagination without having to retype every time we do this rearranging. As we begin to get the objectives and points together in the right order (or at least in an order that suits us), we can then begin to add the facts needed to make necessary points. Some like to use different color cards again for the facts, to distinguish them from the objectives and key points. Here again, the cards give us a look at the way things are shaping up as to length and content behind each objective. We have the same flexibility as before.

After we have arranged the key points and a list of facts we will need in the order in which they will be presented, we can begin to "think" about a final typing—think about, but not yet really finalize! The outline will be complete only if we take care of the testing to see if the students have met the objectives. Most teachers who use the card system for outlining like to have yet a different color card; on these, they write a test item(s) for that objective. This isn't necessarily a part of the outline, but while we have the cards out, with the objectives and associated points and facts, this is a perfect time to make up a question or test for that information. When it comes time for testing, we can "pull" these cards and feel confident that the testing is directly related to the material being presented—if we stick to our outline, that is. It has been stated that test items or questions are an "operational definition" of objectives. This being true, the questions or test items will help clarify the content needed to achieve the objectives, let alone perhaps the objective itself.

When we have done the test questions, and feel that what we have done will meet the objectives, then we can do the final typing. The outline by this time has been tested enough to give us confidence in it and assures us that the lecture will meet the objectives set. We should not have to make any more changes in the outline after we type it this last time. If, at a later date, we feel the lecture needs some changes, something added or updated, or something left out to make room for something else, we have only to get our cards out, decide if we still like the objectives, and make changes. We may have to retype the outline, but the changes will come easy in the cards. Getting comfortable with the use of the cards will save us time and give us a much more orderly presentation, when finally we find ourselves in front of the students with our lecture.

G. *Summary*

The lesson plan should provide for a summary of the material to be taught in the lecture. A good way to do this is to actually write a summary for each of the objectives written for the lecture. For any one hour of lecture, there won't be too many objectives, so the task isn't difficult. It is helpful, though, since this is the last chance we have to make sure we have kept our contract with the students. The summary should be a brief statement or two restating the key thoughts, ideas, or points made in the lecture. The test of how well we have done in preparing the information so far is to see if we find ourselves having to add new facts or not. If we can look at our outline or the cards and decide that here are the things we have taught, and all the information is there, then we have done a good job. If we have to add some

things, put in another key point or two, or re-emphasize
something because we are afraid the point made in the lecture is too weak, then we have found out that the planning
wasn't done very well. *We should do the planning over, not
just decide to teach the points in the summary.* If we didn't
teach it in the body of the presentation, we aren't very likely
to do it in the summary.

H. *Testing*

The lesson plan should tell us just how the testing is to
be done. The actual tests do not need to be in the lesson
plan, but since it is a "plan," we ought to ask ourselves what
our *testing plans* are. We have the tests already taken care of,
but we don't know just how we plan to do the testing, nor
when. Do we plan to have just one major test over all the information or several shorter tests along the way? Do we expect to repeat some of the questions as a means of review and
reinforcing? Do we plan to have short-answer questions or
give subjective-type questions that require more writing and
more time to score? When do we plan to give the tests? During the day, at the end of the day, or the first thing in the
morning? Have we allotted time for the tests? Do we have an
idea of how long the students will need to finish the tests?
(When we get to the section on *Testing* for the lecture, we
will see the answers to these questions.) All of this should be
settled in our minds and in our lesson plans.

Formation of the Lesson Guide

The lesson plan will serve to give us an overview of all that
we plan to do. It will be too massive to use just for lecture
notes or to have in front of us all the time during the lecture.
There is something that will serve us better—a "lesson guide."
This is more like a road map than anything else. It tells us at
a glance just what should be happening at any minute during

the lecture. It is also a quick reference for the aids we need
and the timing. Different people use them in different ways
and design them differently, but most have two essential
ingredients:

1. What the teacher is doing.
2. What the student is doing.

A lesson guide may include a column for the time allot-
ments and another one for the critical aids that are required—
visual or equipment. It can be extended to include key
points, even the objectives. If it gets too lengthy, though, it
begins to be just another lesson plan. The guidebook can include these things, as we have mentioned, including the
copies of the visuals and the reference materials, though we
have suggested that a *reference* to where the reference material can be found will make for a much less cluttered and a
more easily handled guidebook. Below, in Figure 2, is an example of the headings and layout for a typical lesson guide.

Figure 2

Lesson Guide

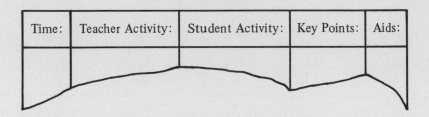

Time:	Teacher Activity:	Student Activity:	Key Points:	Aids:

The important thing to notice about the lesson guide is that
it requires something in *every* column. It keeps us from forgetting that the students may or may not be doing something
if we are lecturing. If we are involved in a straight lecture,
and there are no guided notes or other activities specified for
the students, *we* have to be careful not to say they are

"listening" under the *Student Activity* column. Also, if we
have a title for our lecture and list it under *Teacher Activity*,
and have nothing to put under *Key Points*, we may need to
revisit the lecture and the objectives to see just why we are
giving this portion of the lecture.

Preparation for Presenting the Lecture

Now that the "preparation" is done, we are getting close
to the lecture itself—close, but not quite ready. We have to
prepare ourselves for going before the students—who are real
—to a classroom—which is real, and start to talk. We need to
prepare *ourselves* and *the room*. There is not much we can do
toward preparing the students. Let's look at each of these
"other preparations" separately.

A. *Stage Fright*

For the new lecturer, stage fright is a real thing. There is
the nervousness that comes without warning, just from *thinking* about going before a group of people. The palms of the
hands may get sweaty; there are strange feelings in the stom-
ach; panic seems only a step away; the mind seems to go
blank. It is not logical nor is it pleasant, but it happens to
many even after having done several lectures. We can avoid
some of this trauma, though, and with a little self-analysis,
we can come out on top in such a way that the students will
never know that we had a problem. Part of the solution
comes in our ability to "psych ourselves up" for the
occasion.

There are some physical things that will help us to relax
and gain confidence. One key to relaxing may seem difficult
at first, and that is the need to learn to move around. We may
find ourselves glued to the speaker's stand and our notes. We
are afraid to move for fear we will lose our place or that our
knees won't hold us up. The longer we go without moving,

the harder it will be, and the more tight we get. The move doesn't have to be a giant one, leaping across the room, or encircling the room. Just a step to the side, a movement of the hand or backing up and releasing the speaker's stand will begin to do the job for us. The movements should be *positive* movements, not just weak things that look and feel half-hearted. They should be emphatic, perhaps to emphasize a point. The more positive they are, the more confidence they give us, and the more confidence students will have in our ability to handle class activity. The weaker the movements, the more likely we are to lose our confidence, and this will even come through to the class at times. After we have gotten some confidence, we can make even longer forays out in front of the class. When we have reached the point where we can come right out with the students, even lean on one of their desks, or sit on the table for a short time in front of them, we will feel good. We will feel we are in control and the students will grant us that control just from such an act. This isn't a prolonged thing, of course, where we curl up on a table and stay there. It is more symbolic of our confidence and control, and it doesn't need to last but a minute or so. Again, let's note that movements should be positive. Going to the board or the easel or the overhead should be strong movements to generate enthusiasm. We take several strong steps toward the chalkboard, write with authority, turn and make our point to the class, and then move back to the speaker's stand, if we like. We have made our point, accomplished the task of building our confidence, and the next time will be easier.

Breathing is also important in overcoming stage fright. Any kind of anxiety tends to reduce our breath control; and if we don't get the control back, we will have a hard time dealing with our nervousness. The movement we mentioned above will help, and the two often go hand in hand. We have trouble breathing in a relaxed manner, hence we don't feel like moving, then we don't move, and we have trouble breathing properly. Our breathing problems tend to be shortness of breath. We find ourselves almost "panting." The solution to this is simple enough. *Purposely*—even if it means writing ourselves a big note and placing it on the speaker's stand—take several deep breaths before saying or doing anything. These don't have to be noticeable, and won't be as obvious as we may feel they are. The breathing should be deep down into our lower lungs. It should be slow and deliberate. We should concentrate on it. Any time we feel the original nervousness coming back, we simply need to remember to do our deep-breathing again.

Another help for our stage fright problem is building confidence by *practicing ahead of time*. We can even go through our entire lecture, to the extent that we record it on audiotape or video, though this isn't all that is necessary. We should at least practice the opening statements or the introduction until we feel completely sure how we will open the lecture. Perhaps one of the best things we can do is simply *memorize our opening remarks*. The opening should be clear, deal with the subject, offer a reason for the material, and be emphatic. Knowing just exactly what words we will say will go a long way toward giving us the confidence to continue the rest of the lecture. But this isn't all the practicing we need to do. If we will be writing on the board or using an overhead, we need to practice this as well. We need to try our illustrations and see if they can be drawn quickly and accurately. We need to see if the machine works as we think it does, and practice turning it on and off. We need to build confidence by seeing how it *feels* to turn the pages on the easel, or erase the board, or place a transparency on the overhead projector. We don't have to practice the whole lecture to do this. We can go through our slides or transparencies or board illustrations hurriedly so that this part of the lecture will flow smoothly and all we will have to think about is the lecture itself. We will feel at home with the equipment and this won't be an added frustration.

Another confidence-building technique is to remember to find a friendly face at the onset of the lecture. Some people have seemingly built-in frowns, and if we are suffering from stage fright, we will invariably misinterpret this look as being hostile to us. The thing to do is find that person or persons in the room who have a friendly appearance and look more frequently at these faces than at the others. (Good speaking demands that we maintain eye contact with the group, but it doesn't require us to spend all our eye-contact time with people who look like they just finished cactus soup for lunch.) We need to be careful not to spend too much time looking at the friendly, nodding faces and thus misinterpret the mood of the audience. One of the reasons we maintain eye contact is to gain insight into the audience's reception of what is being said. Even though this is often not very reliable, it is better than just looking at one or two people and making decisions on limited input.

In relation to the above, another thing we can do to relieve the tension is to remember and use some of the names of the people in the audience. Even if we don't know anybody when we first arrive at the classroom, we will meet a few or all of them as they come in. We simply make a point of remembering a few of the ones we have chatted with ahead of time, and even a bit of the conversation. Soon after we get started, we can casually mention something, relating it to a discussion that Tom or Joan had with us before class. This works wonders in getting the group on our side, since it appears that we are really a part of the group. Those whose names are called will especially be drawn into the rapport of the situation, and may be that "friendly face" we will be looking for!

Finally, and this isn't last because it is the least important, there is the matter of humor. If we are in the midst of a "stage-fright attack," we probably won't do too well at humor. Until we know our audience a little better and see how they respond, we will do well to stay away from telling jokes. There is not much that will destroy our confidence as quickly and as badly as telling a "sure winner" joke only to have it fall on its face with no laughter at all. The secret to good humor is having a *sense* of humor. This means when to use it, when not to, how the audience will react, and what kind of humor to use. Many think that having a "sense of humor" means being funny with a lot of jokes. But, most humorists work very hard at a sense of timing, and we would do well generally to avoid this altogether.

B. *Preparing the Room*

Lecture rooms can enhance or detract from the success of a lecture. Therefore, we should check the room before the lecture is scheduled to start. It is not a bad idea to have a checklist of things to look at, even if we use the same room all the time. Someone else may have been using it, or some changes may have been made without our knowledge. A few minutes of checking will save a lot of time and perhaps grief later on.

Acoustics in a room are important and should be checked carefully. It is sometimes difficult to do this, since we can't stand in front of the room and talk, then go to the back and see if we can hear. With a little help from someone else, though, we can check it easily enough. Have someone go with us, sit in different places around the room while we speak in our normal—or lower—voice. We should remember that when there is a room full of people, their regular movement will detract some from the acoustics, and their clothes will absorb some of the sound. Some find it helpful to place a small, portable cassette tape player in different parts of the room and record their voices to see how well they can be heard. It is always good to hear our voices on tape, by the way, because we are usually unaware of how we sound. It is a good way to discover and thus to avoid some of our more distracting speech mannerisms.

Light and climate control are equally important to acoustics. If the room is too difficult to ventilate in a short time, we will do well to plan to start the air control system ahead of time. We need to know where the light switches and climate control devices are situated. If we plan to use some kind of projection equipment, this requires a near-darkened room. We should know where the controls are and where the pulls are on the windows. If there is no easy way to darken the room, we should make preparation to move to another room, devise some way to make arrangements for darkening the room, or decide on some other way of presenting the material. If the only way we can ventilate the room is to open the windows, and we require closed windows for projecting, we should realize this ahead of time so that we can make the necessary adjustments.

Visibility is obviously one of the things we should check. The most apparent item to check is whether the students can see whatever it is they are supposed to see. Here, again, we can check this with a little help. Have someone go with us and sit in front as we move from one part of the room to another. Check the visibility by imagining that there are many people in front of us, not just the one person. Will the students have to look round another person in front of them? It may be that an irregular arrangement of the furniture will help; if so, then we need to make that change ahead of time. Is there glare on the screen or the chalkboard? Turn

on the projector and see if we get any reflections, glare, or
distortions. Check on the size of writing needed to be easily
read from the back of the room. We should have checked on
the visuals before making them; but if we haven't, then they,
too, should be checked for readability. As insignificant as
some of these things seem by themselves, together they make
up the whole of our presentation, and should aid—not detract—from what we are saying.

Something as simple as writing on the chalkboard to get a
feel for it is important to those who are successful at lecturing. We should take a piece of chalk, write on the board in
different places, try out the available erasers, and decide if we
need more chalk or a different kind of eraser.

Once we have made the checks noted above, we are ready
for the lecture itself. We should make a final check on the
equipment to be used, if any. This is true of both the demonstration equipment and any audio-visual media we require.
We should know how to operate it, how to make quick adjustments, and how to replace burned out bulbs. We need to
make certain that we have or know where to find extra bulbs,
too. And there is always the matter of extension cords. Even
if there is one in the room already, we have to face the possibility that someone might need one just before we show up
in the room. We need a spare, in other words! When we have
gone over the checklist the last time, made certain everything
we need is there or readily available, then we can breathe a
sigh of READINESS for the upcoming lecture! While not an
exhaustive list, many of the things to check are summarized
in Figure 3.

Presentation of the Lecture

The lecture consists of several parts, namely the *Introduction*, which tells the students where we are going and why,
the *Main Body* of the presentation, which is the substantive

Figure 3

"Preparing the Room" Checklist

Acoustics
- Can students hear from any point in the room at normal and low voice levels?
- Distracting mannerism in speech?

Lighting and Climate
- Location of light switches?
- Location of climate control switches?
- Can windows be opened?
- Can room be darkened?

Visibility
- Can students see chalkboard, screen, demonstrations, etc.?
- Arrangement of desks and furniture?
- Glare on screen or chalkboard?
- Distortion of projections?
- Size of writing on chalkboard, easel, etc.?
- Readability of prepared visuals?
- Use of chalk and erasers?

Lecturing
- A/V equipment check (operation)?
- A/V equipment check (maintenance: bulbs, extension cord)?

---

data and the application of these data to the work or study at hand, and finally the *Summary* or *Conclusion*, which presents no new information but gives the major points without the supporting data. We will look at each of these separately.

A. *Introduction*

The introduction is just that: our introduction to the students. They may know us by name or face or by reputation, but the introduction of the lecture starts us off on a basis that will usually last throughout the lecture. Even if these are our students each day, we still need to think about the beginning of *each* lecture. The purpose of the introduction is several fold. First, we should use it to get *attention*. Our opening may be the most significant words we utter. With these words, we either set the students up to listen, or turn them off for the rest of the time. There are a number of ways of getting attention. We have already discussed the hazards of humor, but if we are good at it and know from past experience that a certain joke or kind of joke always goes over well with this particular class, then humor is a good way to capture their attention. Humor is a hard act to follow, though, and remember, we have a long way to go, so we can't depend on humor to see us through. We may build up some expectations for humor, too, and if we can't follow through, we might disappoint the students. In this situation, it would have been better if we had left humor alone in the first place.

There are other things we can do to gain attention besides joke-telling in the introduction. We can start off by asking a question that is relevant but seemingly without an answer. We can even begin with a quick quiz over the material—a sort of pretest—to make them aware of what they *don't* know. The test shouldn't be seen as a threat, just an "eye-opener" to let them see where we are going. If we plan to use a demonstration of some kind, this is a good place to do something startling or dramatic with the equipment. Many lecturers do the same thing with words; they make a startling statement, one that is controversial and maybe contrary to the accepted beliefs or ideas of the students. It should be something we plan to deal with, of course, and it should be something that we can substantiate or that becomes clear when they see the full extent of the facts about this subject. (NOTE: We can run this into the ground. Not *every* lecture needs to begin this way.)

The introduction should also stress the *reasons for learning* the material to be presented. We establish this in a "selling" way, to get students to want to learn the material, not in a threatening way to make them dread the rest of what we have to say. A good lecturer will establish needs, showing that the students have certain needs that should be met, then convince them that in the next several minutes these needs will be met. Rather than opening with a statement such as, "Today we are going to talk about ...," a better way to start is with something like, "Many of us have difficulty dealing with ..." This establishes the problem and offers a hope of solution. The worst thing we can do, perhaps, is to open with some statement such as, "You had better learn this or you will be sorry . . ." Threats of this kind turn all of us off, and most of us would close our minds just to *spite* the instructor. We don't have to get attention by making threats. If our material isn't good enough or needed enough to stand on its own merits, threatening dire consequences for not learning it won't get the job done.

The ideal way to get attention and show reasons for learn-ing is to state the objectives right from the start. If we think of them as promises or a contract to the students in which we have an equal responsibility, then we are more likely to sell them on the subject. The statement of the objectives set for the course will do the job, usually. "When this class is over, you will be able to ..." is the contract or promise we are making to them. It is not unusual for the instructor to give the students a written set of objectives at the beginning of the class. This becomes the groundwork for the entire lecture and the testing that follow. The students will know what is expected of them and they will know on what to spend their time concentrating. *There will be no surprises at exam time, either.*

To carry this point further, let's note that some teachers like to give the final quiz at the beginning of the class or course, rather than just at the end. Perhaps the best thing to do is to give sample questions of the type that will make up the final quiz. Students will see that there are certain kinds of problems or definitions that will be on the final quiz, and they will appreciate the class time better as a result. If there are certain kinds of explanations they will have to give, they can be studying them all along, rather than trying to cram for them at the last minute. We can let them keep the sample, explaining that there will, of course, be some differences.

Part of the purpose of the introduction in the lecture is to give an overview of the lecture. A brief summary, after presenting the objectives or selling the idea of the importance of the subject, will get things off to a good start. We don't have to be elaborate, nor give any substantive data; just a quick overview of how we will proceed and what we will be spending time on. Here we want to give a step-by-step look at our approach. An outline handed out in the beginning will accomplish the same thing, but it is still good to give a quick overview to offer some confidence in the ability of the students to keep up. It might be a good idea at this time to also explain any unusual expectations that we have for the students. If there are some time frames that will be different from what they might expect, this is the time to tell them. If the methods of teaching this particular subject will vary from what they are used to, we should go over our expectations with them. If there are some reports or readings they need to do that will require allotting time for access of the material, we put this information in the overview. It is a good time to relax them, and nothing that we can do will build their confidence more than to let them know that we don't plan to have any "secrets" from them. We let them know we are going to run an open, friendly, but business-like class. From this, they can see that while we aren't going to let them off without any work, we still will treat them as mature, sincere students. We plan to accept them at face value until they show us otherwise.

Finally, the introduction is a good time to see if there is any need for clarification on anything that we will be covering, or anything the students will be expected to do. Even if we have given them guided notes, an outline, and a written set of objectives, and have covered all of these and our expectations, some persons will still be confused. Just the fact that they haven't spent the time we have on preparation is ample reason for them not to be as well-informed as we are. It doesn't help their learning experience if we decide that they just aren't listening, or that they have less than average intelligence because they can't understand all those "simple" things we have been explaining to them. Our goal is to see that they learn as much as possible, and if further explanation will help them toward that end, we can spare the time. It may not be enough just to ask, "Are there any questions?" They may be so confused they don't even know enough to ask a question. Or, they may even think they *do* understand, so see no need for asking for clarification. We need some way to get feedback from them to find out for ourselves if they have understood what we have been saying. We can't get any simpler than to ask someone, "How about going over how you see the

assignment for this section of the learning experience?" As
we listen, we can follow along in our mind to see how close
the understanding is. This isn't a time-consuming thing. Only
a minute or two will be required to let us know how they
have received what we said. To carry the feedback a step
further, we can go to another student or several more before
we say right or wrong to the answer we got from the first
one. "Is this how you see it?" or "Are there any changes you
would like to make to that answer?" It is not enough for us
to plan on getting the students somewhere with our teaching
effort; the real success is when we really take them with us as
a result of our clarification efforts in the introduction.

B. *Main Body—Substantive*

We mentioned that there are two parts of the main body:
the substantive portion and the application portion. We will
discuss them separately, though they are both part of the
same thing. The main body of the lecture is the bulk of the
instruction and the time usage. We have talked about the introduction and we will talk about the conclusion, but most
of the time and preparation will be on the main portion of
the lecture. No matter how well we have done the introduction and set the students up to learn and have them com-
mitted with promises, if we can't handle the bulk of the lecture, we are going to let them down hard.

This is the time to give out the data collected and the facts
that support the conclusions we hope to draw from this information. Our familiarity with these facts will make us
appear much more confident, and indeed will give us more
confidence. We need to approach the subject in just this way:
confidently. After all, we have prepared for the things we
plan to say. We *know* that the data support our conclusions.
The students may not be familiar with anything we plan to
say, or they may have a great deal of knowledge, but not as

much as we have—nor is it as well studied and organized. In this part of the main body, we give them the hard facts, remembering that facts get boring quickly. We will have to avoid just reading great volumes of data, or even giving it from memory. Facts not only get boring, they aren't retained very well just from a straight lecture. This is the time for us to think back on what was said earlier about attention spans and use the things suggested to keep student interest high.

If we have many facts to cover and if the only way we can present them to the students is to read them, then it may be wiser to use a handout with references on it so that the students can get to the information when they need it. A clearly written and carefully prepared set of handouts, which are referred to in class and used by the students so that they will be familiar with what is on the sheets, will save us a lot of time and keep us from boring the students by giving the material in the lecture. A caution about the use of handouts, though. The likelihood of students using the handout which contains a great many facts is slim. They have plenty of other things to read besides these rather uninviting sets of facts. If we expect them to use the handout sheets after they leave class, we need to let them use the sheets during class to solve some real problems. They should have a chance to do something meaningful with the sheets during classtime, so that they can see the advantage of the material. After the class, they will then be familiar enough with the handouts and will have seen the usefulness of them, so that they will be willing to read and use them. A general rule to follow in preparing handouts is: if they don't use them *in* class, they won't use them *after* class.

If there ever was a place to use visuals, it is during the presentation of great quantities of facts. This helps keep the material from becoming dull for the students. The visuals will allow the change of pace we discussed earlier and increase the attention span considerably. We aren't talking about just printing the information on pieces of paper and then making visuals of fact after fact written out. The visuals need to be the kind that save us time because they let the students grasp facts more quickly. If we want to compare two things, we use a pie chart or a series of bar graphs that show at a glance the relationships that would have taken us many words to explain. We can use color or sizes or shapes to illustrate the points we want to make. As often as possible, the visual should stand alone in what it teaches. Ideally, the students should be able to look at the visual without hearing any words and get exactly the message we want them to have. A good visual will have both words and pictures that say the same things. If we refer to something being 75 percent of a whole, the pie chart should have the three-fourths colored differently from the rest, and should have the number "75%" written beside it. This way they see two different ways of understanding the 75 percent; and if our words from the lectern are saying the same thing, the information will be well reinforced.

In the main body of the lecture, we need to establish our credibility as soon as possible. We do this not only by knowing our material and speaking with an air of confidence, but also by being able to document what we are saying with references to research and other background material. We don't spend all our time doing this. We don't really try to "snow" the students with our knowledge, but we do give enough supporting information to let them know that we have a right to talk about the subject matter on which we are lecturing. We can use handouts for this, but we still need to refer occasionally to some of the back-up data to keep up our credibility. The giving of the reference material also helps those students who have become interested enough to want to pursue the matter further. They can look up the references and not have to ask too many questions in class. We can even refer them to the material, if it looks as though too much time will be used in answering their questions.

C. *Main Body—Applications/Examples*

If we expect the students to come away from the lecture really believing in the material presented, we would do well to provide them with some practical applications and examples of the things we have been saying. After giving them the substantive material, the hard facts, the back-up data, and the resources for more information, we get to the "so what" of the matter. "Based on all these things we have been saying, here is what it really means . . ." We give them some everyday uses of the facts, some application to their lives or to the kinds of problems they may be having someday in the work-world. No matter how well we have developed our credibility to this point, if we give them some practical applications, they will leave the lecture room believing in the subject, and in us, too. Even if the lecture is on theoretical matters, there should be some kind of application for these theories, and we should find them, mention them, and let the students know that even in the theoretical world, the material can be applied to some problem situation. These examples should be more than just some indication that there is some general use of the information. As much as possible, we should try to give concrete examples of how the material is actually being used by someone *right now*. Our research will help us in this area, of course, and we shouldn't think of it as being complete until we can present examples of how the material is being applied in the "real world."

D. *Summary/Conclusion*

There is a well-known old saying about teaching that states, "Tell them what you're going to tell them, then tell them, then tell them what you've told them." This is still true and it is why we have the introduction, the body, and the conclusion. In the introduction, we "Tell them what we're going to tell them," in the body, we "Tell them," and in the conclusion, we "Tell them what we've told them." As we have already said, the body of the lecture is where most of the "meat" is, where all the supporting data are, and where we make the points and substantiate them with reference material. In the summary/conclusion, we give a quick overview similar to what we did in the introduction. There are some basic rules for making the summary/conclusion as meaningful as possible. Let's look at them briefly.

First, we must remember that we have made our points already, so this isn't the place to *prove anything*. If we are still in the "proving" mode, we are still in the main body of the lecture, regardless of what we call it. The difference between a summary and a conclusion is that in the summary we are merely giving a brief look at the key points without the supporting data. In the conclusion, we may be wrapping up some ideas with further emphasis on the "so what." All of the things we have said now lead us to the following "conclusion." In either case, there is no additional proof of anything. We are just putting the finishing touches on the things we have said in a way that the students will see where we were heading and what it all means.

Another basic rule for this portion of the lecture is that we do not introduce any new information. This isn't the place to make points we forgot to make earlier. We have had the time to present ideas and back them up with supporting data. We don't need to do that now. The thing we have to be most careful about at this point is that we don't detract from the body of the lecture where things were presented in logical form, with key points clearly stated and back-up material for all the things we said. If this becomes a long harangue that sounds like we are trying to still sell the points, we are likely to lose the points already made.

We want to make certain that we don't seem to change direction in the conclusion or summary. This isn't the place to offer some alternative directions or ideas. If we have made our points well, then we should stick with them, not offer the students the possibility that they just may find other conclusions than what we have suggested. This will weaken our arguments and serves only to confuse the students. If there are alternatives, we should bring them into the body of the lecture and offer the supporting data and the arguments for and against them. We don't do it in the conclusion or summary.

The summary or conclusion should be short, concise, and forceful. It should be well-organized and presented in A, B, C, 1, 2, 3 form. It is a good time to have notes that are written in exactly that format. We read them off in a precise form, letting the students know that all they have heard ends up right here with these facts. In the beginning or introduction, we suggested that it was good to know the opening lines. It is equally important that we know the *closing lines*. If we have studied them ahead of time, we won't have any trouble getting out of the lecture. If we don't know them, we will fumble for words, stumble around, repeat ourselves, and end on a very unsatisfactory note.

Testing

The subject of testing is a broad and complex one. It is not the intent in this chapter to deal with the construction of test items nor all the ramifications of the various processes we call *testing*. We do want to tie testing into the lecture design, though, and to understand the significance of the testing process in obtaining feedback for the lecturer *and* students.

Constructing a test to cover the lecture should be no problem if we have followed the procedures discussed so far in this book. We have already said that there should be no surprises at test time. This is because we have developed a set of objectives which became promises or a part of the contract with the students. We shared this with them in the beginning, and they have been operating up until this time under the belief that we will test them on the things we promised them they would know and be able to do when the lecture is over. We may have even given them a copy of a typical final exam. They know what to expect and what is expected of them. If we have built in some efforts at feedback along the way with short quizzes or even some oral feedback from the students, they are even more aware of what to expect from the test.

How do we prepare the test? We look at the original objectives and decide what is the best way to measure these goals. If we did our preparation correctly, we would have even prepared the test before the lecture began. Since one of the requirements for a good objective is that it be measurable, we shouldn't have trouble formulating questions that measure the objective. If we do have trouble, then the objective wasn't very good, and we probably won't be able to measure it well. (That's all right, since if it wasn't a measurable objective, it most likely wasn't a *teachable* subject, and we don't want to know the results anyway!) The only variation in the test and the original objectives is that if we find that for some reason, whether for lack of time or a rearranging of priorities, we failed to deal sufficiently with some subject—hence not meeting that objective—we leave that portion off the test.

We want to be sure that the testing is at the level of the learning we were striving for. If we were teaching only at the basic knowledge level and expected the students to be able to quote something back to us, we shouldn't be testing at the comprehension level, where they will be expected to put things in their own words. On the other hand, if we have set an objective that they will reach the application level of learning, we don't test to see if they can simply feed back some facts to us. We will want to see if they can give examples or recognize the situation from examples we give them. The final testing should be of use to both the instructor and the students. The instructor gets feedback on his or her success and can make modifications in the next period when that lecture is given again. It is a good place to check to see how good our planning has been. It is a good place for the students to see one more time how everything fits together. The logic and order of the test can do quite a bit toward letting the students see just how the material fits together. However, *this is not the place to teach the subject.* If we have failed to get our points across before now, we shouldn't hope that the test will do it for us. For those who say that testing is a good way to teach, we can only say that may be so, but there are many better ways, and teaching this way is only a last resort!

Follow-up

We will not always be able to do a follow-up on our teaching, especially after just one lecture, but we need to consider the possibility any time we have a chance. The final test will give us only a look at the short-term memory processes at work. It doesn't tell us what we can expect two weeks or two months later. It gives us some indication of the spread of students, but a follow-up may reveal that the spread has changed considerably. If we have the opportunity, we can do some random sampling of the students who attended certain lectures, even using the same final exam several weeks later. This will give us a good idea of how well the material was retained, and by doing a good test analysis and comparing this with our lecture processes, we can see what was the most effective in causing the students to retain the most information.

Even if we don't give this same lecture again, we can see if certain kinds of visuals are good for specific kinds of instruction, and use them in this manner in a different lecture. The point of this is that we need as much information as possible about how well we are doing, and using a follow-up process of some kind should give us an idea. Then we will have some information on how we can improve. We always should be striving for improvement, no matter how long we have been lecturing, or how good we *think* we are at it.

IV.

OUTCOMES

What we have tried to do so far is to show the different ways of conducting a lecture and how to prepare and deliver one. Much has been said about the importance of following the procedures given, from the establishing of real, measurable objectives, to the final testing to see if these objectives have been met. All that goes in between is also carefully planned in the successful lecture. Many times we have used the expression, "successful lecture." What do we mean by that expression? In this chapter, we will try to make the advantages clear.

1. In the beginning of this book, we defined the lecture as a means of transmitting cognitive/factual data from a teacher to a group of students in an efficient manner. If the instructor is qualified both as to content and expertise in lecturing, there is the outcome of getting this information to the students in an efficient manner and in a highly organized fashion. It is the *organization* we want to deal with here. Very few other teaching methods allow us to present material in such an organized manner as the lecture. We can pick an amount of available time, decide what information we want to cover in that time, and with good planning go from beginning to end. Along the way, we can get the students involved to some degree and we can use other methods, such as equipment demonstrations and audio-visual aids. The only restric-

tion is our ability to organize the material into the time allowed. We will be as organized as our planning permits and to
the extent we follow our notes. If the students are adept at
note-taking, or if we provide them with guided note-taking
means, we can be certain the students will get the information in a completely organized way.

2. If we follow the outline and share the objectives with
the students, and if we provide them with good note-taking
capability, they will have a *good reference for future learning*. Listening to a lecture, even a well-planned and executed
one, will not give the students the best possible recall value,
but the notes and the in-class exposure to the material will
allow them to reflect in their private study. As they see the
notes they have taken and the references to other sources of
information, they can begin to make the information more
permanent in their memories. What we have done for them
is weed out much of the irrelevant data they would have to
go through to get the subject down to the form they have in
their notes. While we have done our research, they only
have to accept our word for it, and can look further if they
like. If we have been precise in our presentation, dealing only
with the critical facts at hand, and avoiding the story-telling
that is interesting but not productive, they can get an accurate and quick overview of the entire subject.

3. Along the same line, their notes will supply them with a
storage bank for locating data other than the specific data
presented to them. Our reference sheets, handouts, and
guided-note references will give them a place to start to expand their information on the material. If we keep this in
mind as we provide them with additional sources, we will give
them an easy-access method of finding more information. We
can stimulate this with some challenging questions, or even
whet their appetites with a wisp of exciting data that lies
right around the corner with a little more research. We really

haven't done our job of teaching if we have satisfied the students when we terminate our in-class teaching. The good teacher hangs out the carrot of excitement for further learning, mostly by letting the students learn a little of that information as an added incentive.

4. The lecture offers an easy way to *make and fulfill some learning promises*. If we establish the objectives properly and then plan and carry out the lecture according to the best way of reaching these objectives, we can let the students see that they, in fact, reached the prespecified goal. The difference between just another dull lecture and a rewarding experience often is the excitement of *learning something*. Few things motivate students more than simply knowing they have learned. This is why we have to be more than casual in our planning. Think of the reward when the teacher says, "here's what you will be able to do when this teaching session is over," then at the end to find that they actually can do it! There is little that will bring students back to the trough quicker than this kind of experience. Again, it says that we *have* to have some objectives, that we make an honest effort to meet them with the students, and that we have a measuring device that lets the students (and ourselves) know that they have been met.

5. One of the possible outcomes of the successful lecture is the securing of emotional or attitudinal changes within the learners. Most lectures are not designed to work in the affective domain, but few lecturers go very far without their own personalities showing through. This means their prejudices and biases also show through. Whether we like it or not, whether we intend for it to happen or not, our biases will likely be passed on to the students. This isn't all bad, of course. We have enough information to convince us that a certain thing is right. In our presentation of the information, this belief will come out. It is possible that many will leave

the lecture inclined in their beliefs the same way. If we have strong enough convictions on the matter, we may even *plan* on this happening. The caution here, obviously, is to do our persuading with logic, reasoning, and supporting data, not with emotion alone. Just "preaching" on the subject and spending more time on the subject than it is worth may have the opposite effect. We may drive students away from our position rather than closer to it. The lecture is a good way to deal with this kind of effort, because it gives us an uninterrupted platform. If we expect the students to really believe in what we have been trying to convince them of, and to go away telling others, they will have to do some verbalizing and testing on their own. This can be done after we have presented our case with the necessary back-up data.

6. One major outcome for the instructor is that the lecture provides a quick and accurate way of *evaluating the success of the teaching process*. We know where we want to go. We establish objectives that tell us this. We decide how we want to get there. Our lesson plans give us plenty of help in this direction. We operate in a controlled environment, since the lecture is essentially under the lecturer's control. We even decide ahead of time how we will measure the success of our efforts. When we put all of this together, we have rather conclusive evidence on just how well things went. If our testing is any good at all, we can even do some minute analysis of what went well and what did not go so well. We ought to be able to tie specific questions to certain times in the lecture and to things we were doing at the time. While this might not work so well in helping with the present class—they have had their chance at this lecture—it tells us what we can expect the next time we give the same lecture. Further, it may tell us of weaknesses within the students and may help us to set some prerequisites for future attendees. We may well want to go back and look at our lesson plan and see if we spent too

much time on certain areas (since most students got all the answers without trouble) or see if we spent too little time on other areas (since many did badly in certain areas). We may change some of our objectives as a result; adding more or removing some of them. We may even want to look at the testing program. Since we have such a controlled environment, all of these things are possible and perhaps necessary for future success in lecturing.

V.

DEVELOPMENTAL GUIDE

We have tried to point out all the steps in preparing the successful lecture. Since so much learning in the world is still done in this format, it behooves us to think carefully about it and not take it for granted. Even when we know the subject and have lectured for a long time, planning is still required. The following steps are suggested in preparing for any lecture.

1. *Know the students*. No matter what kind of planning we do, if we fail to take the students into consideration, not much good is likely to result, and what does will be accidental. We need to find out all we can about the students. What are their backgrounds? What are their success records in learning? Have they been exposed to this subject matter content previously? If so, with what results? What have past students done with the information we are about to teach? Have the students changed from one time to the next? Will they have any problems with this subject or with me as the lecturer? Does the course have a "reputation"? What other things will they be doing besides coming to my lecture? All of this comes under the heading of *student analysis* (described later in this chapter), as does information on how they will use the information. Will they have an opportunity to apply the information after they leave me, or is this the last they will have to deal with the data?

2. *Establish objectives.* It is possible that for one lecture we may not go to the trouble of deciding just what the students will be able to do when the lecture is over, but we can be sure that if we get into the habit of doing this, our students will suffer. We will also lose the advantages mentioned in the previous chapter of this book. We won't be able to measure our successes nor be able to fulfill promises made to the students. This is an important consideration—and something not to be dealt with lightly. In writing the objectives, we simply ask ourselves, "What do I want them to be able to do at the end of the lecture that they can't do now? Can I measure it? Is it possible for them to get there in the time allowed?" The answers to these questions will allow us to specify firm objectives that will become promises or part of our contract with the students.

3. *Plan the lesson.* After we have looked at the students and decided where we would like them to be at the end of the lecture, we set about to plan how to get them there. The lesson plan is just that: a plan of how the lesson will go. It tells us what we will be doing and when we will be doing it. It tells us what equipment we will be using, and what we will be doing with it. The lesson plan includes the visuals we plan to use along with any exercises in which the students will be involved. It also tells us what the students will be doing at any given time. It provides us with back-up references, supporting data, and an outline of the entire presentation. It will also tell us what kind of testing we will do and when we will do it. It is only a plan, though, and we will choose either to use or not use it. If it is a good plan, we should make every effort to use it.

4. *Prepare the lesson guide.* The lesson plan sets out direction. The guide is the road map to follow in getting where we are going. The lesson guide has the final outline of the lecture, copies of the tests, copies of the visual aids, copies of

the most important reference materials, and any additional notes we write to ourselves. It may include some thought questions to stimulate the students during dull periods. It will include copies of the exercises and handouts we plan to give to the students. It is so complete that someone else could conceivably pick it up and, provided they had the background knowledge, go through with the lecture as we had planned. In fact, that is the way we should think of the lesson guide: a guide for anyone who will be giving this lecture at any time. Even if we are away from the subject for a long period, the fact that we have the guide should shorten our preparation time when we are ready to give the lecture again. It will take some time in the beginning, but the time it saves may be our own some day!

5. *Prepare for the presentation.* Depending on our previous experience, preparing for the presentation may be no more than a refresher of the material, the guide, and the facilities. On the other hand, it may be that we will have to spend several hours practicing in front of the mirror, memorizing portions of the lecture, especially the first part, then more time in the classroom checking it out. Normally, we will at least know our opening remarks well, be familiar with the procedures we have planned, know when and how to use the demonstration equipment and audio-visual media, and know that the room is properly set up acoustically and sight-wise. We will also know our closing remarks so that the lecture will end on an upbeat.

6. *Present the lecture.* The crux of the matter lies in our efforts to go before the students and present that which we have planned to deliver. Our presentation consists of the introduction, which tells them what to expect, including any promises and procedures we want to give them. Then comes the main body of the lecture, which is the heart of the whole design in which we present the facts, supporting data, and

any applications and examples we plan to use. Finally, there is the conclusion or summary which wraps up the things we have said without giving the supporting data.

7. *Do the testing.* The measure of success for both the instructor and the students lies in the final testing efforts. It is here that we find out if promises have been kept and if the objectives have been met. There should be no surprises at testing time. We have told the students what to expect, perhaps even given them copies of sample final tests, and now they will be tested. It should come as a normal part of the lecturing/teaching/learning process. The students should expect testing to tell them how they have done, and there should be no surprises on the results of the scoring.

8. *Follow-up on the results.* If it is possible to do so, we should find a way to do some kind of follow-up on how well the students did on the material we taught them. Since forgetting happens rather quickly, usually within the first few days, we can do a random sampling on the class using the same final examination if necessary, and see how much they remember in the elapsed time. This will allow us to examine our procedures and make variations not only in this same lecture the next time, but also in other lectures if we find that one kind of approach works better for us than another.

The above has outlined the general developmental steps, the details of which have already been presented in previous chapters. In the Design Format chapter, we mentioned that there is a need to analyze the student population before going into a series of lectures. The importance of such an analysis cannot be stressed enough. Because of its importance, the following is intended to detail what is required in such an analysis. As part of development, indeed a key beginning point, it is important that we detail the requirements at this time.

Student Analysis

Any time we take on a new group of students, we should do our best to know some things about them. The effectiveness of our lecture effort may be directly proportional to what we are able to learn about our listeners. While *student analysis* isn't a direct part of the lecture method of instruction, we have added it to this chapter, as it relates to development (and implementation). In an earlier chapter, we listed six things that we need to find out about the students before we face them.

1. *Age distribution*. We can tell a lot about people just by knowing their age. For example, we know that those people who grew up during the Depression have a certain general viewpoint toward things like money, savings, waste, etc. People who were born in the early 1950s probably had much more, without having had to work as hard for it, and feel much differently about using money to solve problems.

If our class is comprised of working people, they will be more serious, more concerned about accountability, maybe even exhibit less confidence in themselves, especially if they haven't been in class for some time. Full-time students will be accustomed to attending class and may appear to be less concerned about how well they do. People who are on some kind of tuition plan and have to make certain grades will press harder, ask more questions, be more disturbed at testing time, and be less tolerant with poor teaching. Those who don't have to give account for their grades frequently will be less worried about testing and the fairness of the testing. Employees within an organization are quite different from those in the academic world, thinking almost entirely about application on their immediate job. These people will generally be older than those in the academic world.

Suppose there is a mixture in ages? Frequently there is, and we need to know that. If there is, then what we know is that we can't design instruction that will suffice for the entire class. We have to be flexible and handle different people in different ways. Perhaps a better way of looking at it is to say that we have to be prepared with different designs to meet most of the situations presented by a variety of ages.

2. *Previous learning experiences.* If we know something about previous experiences—successes and failures—we can design our lectures with more accuracy. Attitudes toward learning are directly related to the experiences people have had with other learning efforts. The degree to which they *think* they can learn something is the degree to which they actually can learn it, for the most part. Our chances of changing attitudes are fairly slim. If they have developed a poor attitude about their ability to learn something, we will have to work hard at changing it, and even then it is a long, hard struggle. We aren't likely to do it by things we say in the lecture, but by things that *happen* to the learners in the class.

Let's look at some examples of how previous learning experiences can affect a student in a class. If the students have experienced much success at learning, and if challenges have been met with solutions almost every time, with little outside help, then we have a group of students who are ready to learn anything we throw at them. They are used to difficult situations in the classroom as far as learning is concerned and can get excited about the prospects of another challenge. Learning is no threat to them and they see the instructor as an aid, not an obstacle, to their learning. They may or may not feel a need for the teacher to contribute to the learning process. They may just want direction to where to find the resources, and the lecture we give may be no more than suggestions for finding additional information. They won't feel any distress if we don't hold their hand during the learning process. They may feel more of a threat if we give them too much guidance and look over their shoulder all the time. Their past history of learning has assured them that they have the capability, and so they are ready to learn. Our job is to make certain that they do.

In preparing our lectures for this kind of class, we try to develop the material in logical ways, using reasoning as much as possible, and allowing for both inductive and deductive thought processes from the students. We use a lot of open-ended statements and questions. We keep the group busy with drawing their own conclusions. We set up the problem and they find the solutions. We challenge their thinking, showing that we respect their intelligence. We use that intelligence and their habit of thinking things through to get the learning taken care of, and this continues to build their confidence in themselves and their learning ability. This group doesn't need many successes to motivate them to continue. They don't have to be told along the way how well they are doing. They expect to do well and they will know how well they are doing at any given time. If they don't, they will probably ask, but won't be discouraged if they aren't where they think they should be. They will just work that much harder to get there. The challenge provides the motivation for this group. They do need some success somewhere, though, and it needs to be a big one to make the effort worthwhile. In summary, we can say that when we know that the group is one that has had good experiences and large amounts of success at learning in the past, then we should see that they have challenges to motivate them, and some frequent but large rewards or successes at the end of their efforts.

How about the students who have not had much success at learning? How do we treat them? This is quite a different group and we are fortunate if we know about them in advance. We tailor our lecture and learning activities quite a bit differently with them. They have seen learning activities as a threat during most of their learning experiences. Even the classroom itself, and certainly the teacher, are representative of unpleasant and unsuccessful experiences from their past. Because their success rate is low, they generally *expect* to do poorly, or even to fail. They come waiting for the first indication to *not* understanding something, so they can say to themselves—and maybe to us—"See, I told you I couldn't learn this." They have had few successes and rarely ever have been able to handle challenges. They make no distinction between "challenge" and "threat."

In preparing learning activities for the lecture to this group, we don't depend on their reasoning power to make up the difference between what we say and the end product of learning. We have to lead them step-by-step to successes. We don't necessarily do all the talking, but we see that they talk about things that they can understand, and we lead them to statements with careful planning. When we ask them a question, it should have an obvious answer, especially early in the learning experience. To surprise them with a challenging question right at the beginning of the lecture will do about as much as anything to bring their learning experience to an end during this lecture period and maybe for those yet to come. This is a good time to get them working on assignments in small groups, so that no one person is overly threatened. If the answer is correct to the question we ask, the person answering feels lifted, and the rest of the group working with that person can feel some satisfaction for being the ones that furnished the right answer. If the answer is wrong, then the person can blame it on the rest of the small group and not feel as bad as if he or she had come up with the incorrect answer alone. Of course, working in small groups, pooling information, and talking about the problem will increase the likelihood of their getting the correct answer anyway. Assignments for this group should be clear and without any "tricky" alternatives. It is helpful if we actually go part way with them into the assignment, letting them see that they can do it, and that it isn't something that will require them to be geniuses. At the same time, we can't go around telling them that this is disgustingly simple and that they should be ashamed to be working on something this easy. We want to build their confidence as much as possible, though it will obviously take a long time, and we may not be able to accomplish it in the time we have. They have had a long time to lose their confidence in the ability to learn, and probably little help along the way from various teachers, so the task is a difficult one. Fortunately, we can build some confidence for learning in *our* class. We should concentrate on this challenge first and not try to reshape their whole outlook on learning.

Since they have gone for much of their learning life without much success at learning, the most obvious thing we can aim for is to give as much chance for success as possible. The good part about this is that the successes don't have to be large ones. They do have to be frequent, though, to keep the confidence level from slipping any lower than it probably is already. For the most part, we can't fully imagine just how these people feel about learning, but we can formulate and use small amounts of success to motivate them. In fact, there is no way they can appreciate large successes. They will see small learning achievements as big anyway, so we just plan to allow them to experience frequent successes, but keep them as small as we like. It may be no more than asking them to repeat something we have just said, or reading from the right place in the book. Gradually we expand on this, of course, to the point that they are taking bigger and bigger steps.

Even with the tests we give, it helps if we consider the kinds of learning experiences the students have had. Successful students usually don't worry about the test questions, except for making certain they are fair and not tricky. They are concerned about their grades, but only to make sure they live up to their own expectations. In their case, we generally don't have to worry too much about the order of the questions or the degree of difficulty. With the less than successful students, this is not the case at all. Tests have usually been the way they find out about their failures. Taking tests is the most painful part of the teaching-learning situation for them. Very little good has ever been experienced in the taking of tests. If they expect to fail in the course, they expect to do especially poor at test time. The only surprise for them at test time is to be able to answer questions on the test correctly. We have to change that for them. We have to make testing more comfortable and allow them to get answers correct; expecting to do so! There should be no surprises at test time as to content anyway, no matter what kind of students we have, and this group is especially sensitive to questions over material not covered or only inferred. What we do is first build their confidence during the lecturing and teaching activities. Then, let them deal with the same kind of questions that will be on the test. They get a chance to ask questions, delve into the subject covered in the test in detail, knowing they are discussing possible test questions. We don't teach the test, but we make certain that they know what will be on the test and what we expect from them as they take it.

The structure of testing is significant for the students who haven't enjoyed success at learning. About the worst thing that can happen is to open up the test, look at the first question, and not know how to deal with it. For this group, the best possible thing is to be able to answer the first question they see. This tells us that we save the more difficult questions till further in the test, putting the easier ones toward the beginning.

The design of the test instrument is important, too. Any question on the test should be easily understood, but especially so with this group. We have to be careful that the wording or construction of the question doesn't get in the way of finding out if the student knows the answer. In all too many tests, the students miss the *question*, not the answer. It ought to be obvious to these students when they have answered a question correctly, too. Simple, single-word answers are better and more rewarding than long, multi-faceted answers that may or may not be correct, and may be only judgmental as to the degree of rightness or wrongness. The conclusion, then, is that for the students who haven't had much success at learning, the tests should be simple, over material that has been well-studied in class, and the answers they are most likely to know should be for questions asked early on the tests.

3. *Prerequisite learning levels.* We have seen that it is helpful to know in advance the degrees of success the students have had in their learning life. They also bring something with them we call their "prerequisite learning level." This is a composite of what they know about any particular subject, their comfort level with the subject, their readiness to learn more about that subject, and the amount of knowledge they have compared to where we plan to start the subject we are teaching. Note that this is more than just knowing their *knowledge* level. It includes knowing their *readiness to use* what they know, as well as the foundation for the new learning experience. Knowing this ahead of time allows us to decide how much motivation we have to provide for the particular subject we are talking about. We also need to know how comfortable they are with the content, meaning that we should know if they see some value in the materials, feel they can handle the subject, and can relate to it in a satisfactory way instead of struggling to find just why they are in the class at all. None of this is a measure of how well they can learn or if they can learn this particular subject matter. We need to know that, too, but just because they *can* learn

something we have no guarantee that they *will* learn it. Their prerequisite learning level will tell us more about whether they will or won't learn. In fact, if we know what they have already learned, how they feel about this subject, and where to start teaching them, we can predict the degree of success they will have. Knowing what they have already learned tells us most of what we need to know about their ability to learn. We know that they can handle the material that is similar to what we are going to be lecturing on; that they have had enough experience with the subject not to be afraid of tackling more of it; and that they aren't coming into this course or lecture blindly. That is much more than just knowing what scores they have made on a pretest of some kind.

If we know the prerequisite learning levels of the students, we can prepare for the lecture more easily, making plans to either start out immediately with the subject matter, or going more slowly with some stage-setting. If they are not comfortable with the content, we may need to deal with some motivational things ahead of time. We may have to show the application of what we are getting ready to teach, or show some examples of where others have used the content to accomplish other things. If we can know these things when the students arrive, it saves us from having to find them out after we start, and this saves us considerable time.

4. *Acceptance of the teaching-learning environment*. Many learners are "socially-oriented" learners, and are affected by the learning environment as much as the content or the instructor. Their propensity for learning changes with the social environment where the learning is taking place. This isn't "social" in terms of just the kind of people who are in the class and how well they get along with each other. We need to know if these are the kinds of students we are going to have. If so, we know that the success will not only depend upon how well we lecture, but also on how the students interact with

each other. It also indicates that the instructional design is going to need some kind of student involvement. If there are not chances to work with the other students in the class, then they will find the learning experience frustrating and unrewarding. With the right student-student or student-instructor interaction, it will be a rewarding experience for them. There is evidence to show that these kinds of students tend to "flock" together, taking all the same learning opportunities, for the obvious reason of being together. There is no evidence to show that they are inferior students, nor that they cause any kind of problems. They work hard and enjoy it, if the conditions are right. It is just a case where the learning *activity* is an end in itself, rather than a means to an end.

There are other students, naturally, who don't have this social need. They must be dealt with quite differently to make the experience meaningful to them. For example, there are some students who are careful to pick learning opportunities based on what they can *get as a result of the learning*. They see the learning as a means of getting them to some desired goal, and they want to learn for that reason. They don't object to the social aspects of the learning, but they would if they felt it was a barrier in any way to their learning. Their motivation comes from seeing the goal about to be attained. They will be more interested in getting the course behind them, though they don't mind doing whatever it takes to get there. They are skillful learners but generally do not question the way a thing is being taught. They may question *why* they have to learn something and will be satisfied only if the goal they are seeking is found in the reason for learning. They will be less tolerant of those things that are superfluous to their goal. Since learning is a means of getting them to some end, the motivation will not be the learning itself, but the anticipation of the goal. When we are teaching a group such as this, we must orient our lecture toward results to be acquired *after*

the learning is over, rather than just stick with the learning itself. If we don't know we have these people in the class, we
may spend too much time preparing the lecture on the content as an end in itself, rather than build in some application
for the learning.

There is another group of students that actually find that
learning is an end in itself. They enjoy the acquisition of
knowledge and get their motivation out of learning. They are
not all that excited about the application, except that hearing
about it may be a *learning experience* for them. Neither are
they interested in the *process* used in the teaching-learning
activity. Whatever helps them suits them fine. When we
design a class for these students, we have to concentrate more
on the learning than anything else. We also have to let them
know they have learned. Since the learning is the end in itself, they must know that the learning is taking place. They
will look forward to feedback devices, whether questions or
activities, that give them the information on how well they
are learning. We can best prepare this group by introducing—
in our first remarks—how much learning and what kind of
learning will take place, and how they will know that they
have learned.

The obvious observation at this point is that we may well
find all of these types of students in our classes. What do we
do? If we know this ahead of time—and that is the point of
this section—we can make arrangements for *all three* to be
satisfied. There is no one kind of lecture that will satisfy all
of these learners, but we can build something in for each.
We can have sub-group activity and other interaction exercises for the learners who need the social climate in the classroom; we can offer opportunities for applications and build
in examples frequently enough to convince the goal-oriented
learners that there is something for them after the learning is
over; and we can offer frequent evidence that learning is

taking place for those who find their motivation in the learning itself. None of these kinds of students will mutually exclude the others, so we don't have to worry that one method will satisfy one or two of the types, but discourage the other.

5. *Student reasons for taking the course.* Obviously, students take various courses and classes for many different reasons. Their reasons may or may not be known, but it helps if we can find out some of the typical reasons people are taking the classes where we are lecturing. In the previous section, we discussed types of learners. In this discussion, we are not talking about types of students and their expectations, but rather the reasons any particular student takes this specific class at this particular time. The same student, taking the same class will be quite a different student if the reasons for taking the class change. It is most important that we find out as much as we can about the reasons for the students being in our lecture sessions. Otherwise, we may misunderstand or misinterpret actions by the students. If the student is in the class as a requirement, then we will have a much different student than one who has chosen this class on the basis of personal interest, perhaps even over another class option. Students who end up in any class for reasons other than a personal, first-choice basis are going to have different attitudes toward the learning activities from those who have come on a voluntary basis. If they perceive of themselves as having gotten "stuck" with us, they are not going to be too anxious to go through the exercises we propose, do the assignments, or listen to the lectures. They will dread examinations—what is going to be on them—not from wanting to know the material but to pass the test and escape. If, on the other hand, we can show them that the course isn't all that bad, that they can learn and even enjoy it, that the material has some application to what they are involved in, then we can change their outlook toward the material. It will be our job, not theirs, to

accomplish this, and the more we can know ahead of time, the more likely we will be able to accomplish it.

6. *Likelihood of success as seen by other instructors*. Our final bit of helpful information can come from those instructors who have taught the same students we are getting ready to instruct. Up until now, we have done as much as we can to find out about the students' readiness to learn and their preparation and previous knowledge. Now we want to see what other instructors can tell us about these particular students, especially as they sat in "their" class and participated in "their" learning process. We are not just interested in students' attitudes toward teachers and learning, but rather their likelihood of success as viewed from the standpoint of teachers who have actually tried to put them through learning assignments. This is obviously valuable information and not difficult to obtain. We have to keep reminding ourselves that it isn't the students' attitudes we are interested in but the likelihood of achievement in our class. Sometimes, teachers get the two confused, thinking that a person with a sullen or disinterested countenance is equivalent to being a poor risk as a student. Experienced teachers have learned that this isn't always the case and that frequently, those who *appear* to be the most interested are often the least likely to succeed. They are eager to be a part of the learning activity, but don't have the ability to handle the material or the necessary concentration capability to follow the lectures.

Conclusion. So, what have we learned? We have found that there are some things that are available to us in the way of existing facts that will help us to do a better job with our students. This information is available to us from various sources, but we need to seek it out. To fail to find out some things about our prospective classes is to be willing to do a less than average job of teaching. We have the capacity to improve the quantity and quality of the learning that takes place by finding out certain things about the students with regard to their age, previous learning experiences, prerequisite learning levels, acceptance of the teaching-learning environment, their reasons for taking the course, and the likelihood of success as viewed by other instructors. The question that arises is, What if each class consists of a mixture of all of these different levels we have talked about? The answer is two-fold: First, what would I have done if I hadn't known these things about the class? Second, I must build into the course some or all the things the individuals need to meet their different backgrounds, learning levels, and so on. True, we can do this anyway, even without knowing the class, but we are more likely to be accurate in our teaching if we know as much as possible ahead of time. If we have classes that are predominantly one way, it will change our design considerably. While we don't just teach for the majority, we can *design* for the majority, letting the rest of our teaching be varied enough to take care of the smaller groups. Of course, we can just ignore the make-up of the class, and do what we would normally do with any class at any time, doing whatever comes "naturally" for us. In this case, we must hope that we are "naturally" good, since that is the only hope the students have. The alternative—and the one the good instructors invariably take—is to take advantage of any edge they can get to improve the possibility of the teaching-learning situation being even a *little* better. With enough effort along these lines, the learning turns out to be *considerably* better.

VI.

RESOURCES

BOOKS

Anderson, R. H. *Selecting and Developing Media for Instruction.* New York: Van Nostrand Reinhold, 1976; and Madison, Wisconsin: American Society for Training and Development.

Broadwell, M.M. *The Supervisor as an Instructor.* Reading, Mass.: Addison-Wesley, 3rd edition, 1978.

Craig, R.L. (Ed.) *Training and Development Handbook.* New York: McGraw-Hill, 1976 (sponsored by the American Society for Training and Development).

Gagne, R. *The Conditions of Learning.* New York: Holt, Rinehart, and Winston, 1965.

Kozma, R.B. *et al. Instructional Techniques in Higher Education.* Englewood Cliffs, New Jersey: Educational Technology Publications, 1978.

Laird, D. *A User's Look at the Audio-Visual World.* Fairfax, Va.: National Audio-Visual Association, 1974.

Mager, R. F. *Developing Attitudes Toward Instruction.* Palo Alto, California: Fearon, 1968.

McKeachie, W. J. *Teaching Tips: A Guidebook for the Beginning College Teacher.* Lexington, Mass.: D. C. Heath, 1969.

Nadler, L. *Developing Human Resources.* Houston: Gulf, 1970 (supported by the National Society for Training and Development).

Neimark, M. *Personality Orientation*. Englewood Cliffs, New Jersey: Educational Technology Publications, 1976.

Rigg, R. P. *Audio-Visual Aids and Techniques*. London: Hamisch Hamilton, Ltd., 1969. (Distributed in the United States by Olympic Film Service, 161 West 22nd Street, New York, New York 10011.)

Skinner, B.F. *The Technology of Teaching*. New York: Appleton-Century-Crofts, 1968.

Warren, M.W. *Training for Results*. Reading, Mass.: Addison-Wesley, 2nd edition, 1979.

ARTICLES

Broadwell, M. M. The Use and Misuse of A-V. *Training*, October 1970, p. 40.

Davis, J., and J. Hagaman. What's Right—And Wrong—With Your Training Room Environment? *Training*, July 1976, p. 28.

Deterline, W. A. The Secrets We Keep from Students. *Educational Technology*, February 15, 1968, 7-10.

Randall, J. S. You and Effective Training—Part 5: Methods of Teaching. *Training and Development Journal*, October 1978, 8-11.

I Like It When Teachers Are ... *Learning*, February 1979, 7(6), 46-47.

Why Some Group Discussions Are Duds. *Techniques*, April 1975, 15(6).

SEMINARS

Effective Classroom Instruction. Applied Management Institute, Walnut Creek, California.

How to Improve Classroom Training Techniques. University of Michigan, Ann Arbor, Michigan.

VII.

APPENDIX A

A GUARANTEED FAILURE SYSTEM FOR LECTURING

It would seem that some, by their actions, are determined to fail at lecturing. No matter what is said to them, or what they might read in a book, by ignoring all helpful hints they manage to do a very poor job of teaching using the lecture method. In many cases, they seem to even work at it and continue their poor performance for years, as though there was a cheering crowd urging them on. Be this as it may, the purpose of this Appendix is to *help these people toward their chosen goal of failure*.

The following description and checklist is a time-tested way of guaranteeing a very unsatisfactory job of presenting material, teaching students, and getting in the way of learning. *NOTE:* While there will be some who read and say that they don't fit the prerequisite (i.e., they don't intend to fail at lecturing), it might be a good idea to read this anyway. Some have discovered that their actions fit some of the things, though their intent was not to do a poor job of lecturing. There may be something here for all of us!

Check (√) appropriate box:

I DO: I DON'T:
( )   ( )   1. I like to go into a lecture without too much preparation. That way, I have a fresh approach and a more relaxed lecture. (There may be times when going in without much preparation will give us a "relaxed" air; but if we do this very often, the end product is a sloppy lecture, a disorganized presentation, and learners who are quite confused as they try to take notes and learn.)

91

I DO: I DON'T:
( )   ( )   2. I like to show up right at the last minute so the
                        students will be ready to get down to business
                        and we won't spend a lot of time on irrelevant
                        things before starting. ("Irrelevant things" in
                        this case may be things like getting notes in or-
                        der, checking out the room for distractions and
                        acoustics, and giving the students a chance to
                        get seated before starting.)

I DO: I DON'T:
( )   ( )   3. I feel a good knowledge of the subject is still
                        the key to success in teaching, rather than wor-
                        rying about methods. If I know my material
                        well enough, I can get it across to the students
                        regardless of how I teach. (There are many
                        instructors who come into a classroom with a
                        great deal of information, and when they leave
                        they still have it. None of it has been imparted
                        to the students. A knowledge of the subject is a
                        primary requirement, but knowing what to do
                        with it in a teaching-learning situation is *equally
                        primary.*)

I DO: I DON'T:
( )   ( )   4. I feel that students are conditioned to listening
                        to lectures, and any use of visual aids or illustra-
                        tions in my lectures is just time-consuming and
                        distracting to the students. (No doubt, students
                        are somewhat conditioned to lectures, but
                        every indication we have about learning says
                        that they still learn better from *seeing* than
                        from *hearing*. Some studies show that as much
                        as 75 percent of what we learn is the result of
                        something we have seen.)

I DO: I DON'T:
( )   ( )   5. I like to keep the students alert by calling on
                        unsuspecting students on sort of a "fast-draw"
                        question basis. They are sometimes shocked
                        and embarrassed, but it keeps them awake.
                        (This is a good way to be remembered by the
                        students, the same way we remember ogres,

witches, and monsters ... If we depend upon shock treatments to keep students awake, it tells us something about our ability to keep them awake with just our presentation. Asking questions is a good method, but the purpose ought to be to get feedback, not to keep students awake. We keep them alert with involvement, change of pace, and structured designs, which help them get closer to the learning activity.)

I DO: I DON'T:
( ) ( )   6. I feel that my job is to see that they have the information presented to them. Their job is to get it! (There is some merit to this philosophy, though it always comes out wrong in practice. What happens is that the teacher ends up putting out the information in any way that suits him or her, without regard to learning results. No teacher will ever be completely successful if the goal of teaching isn't to see that learning takes place. Better stated, "My job is to see that the students learn the information/skill. Their job is to do the things I have designed to help that happen.")

I DO: I DON'T:
( ) ( )   7. I think it is important to design the teaching session around the material, not the students, since students change and the material doesn't. (One of the most important questions we can ask ourselves is, "Could we teach this course without the students?" What that means is, if there were no students present, could we still progress through our teaching design? If the design requires students doing something, then our instructional design has a possible chance of success. If we have built the design around stable material rather than around changing students, the chances for success are almost nil.)

I DO: I DON'T:
( ) ( )   8. I believe it is important to get students involved, but only if there is time enough in the

lecture session. Students invariably slow the teaching efforts down when they get involved. (There is no question that we will have a smoother session, cover all the material, and meet a predetermined time frame if we can keep the students out of it. If we want learning to take place, unfortunately, we will have to get them involved. They will disrupt our lesson plan, get us off the track, cause us to have to repeat things they have misunderstood, and make it impossible for us to stay right on schedule. The only justification is that learning will take place better when they get involved.)

I DO: I DON'T:
( )   ( )   9. I feel that every student deserves equal time and should have an equal share of my teaching efforts. (Students are *not* equal, and do not *need* an equal share of the instructor's time. Some students can move on without us, and will be slowed down if we spend too much time with them. Other students need some time to help them over rough spots. This small amount of time will keep them from falling helplessly out of it. If the faster students are turned loose, they won't resent the time spent with the slower students.)

I DO: I DON'T:
( )   ( )   10. I think that any time I try to change the level of my voice, use gestures, or move around, all I'm doing is acting, and that is not the "real me." Sincerity demands that I not "put on" any kind of "show" for the students. (The difference between *putting on a show* and *good teaching* may be no more than understanding the reason why we do some things. It may be natural for us to mumble or write poorly on the board. If we learn to talk clearly or loudly enough to be heard, or learn to write legibly on the chalkboard, that is not *acting*. It is being fair to the students. So it is if we make our voice and actions more meaningful or interesting to the students.)

I DO: I DON'T:
( )   ( )   11. I believe the students who are trying deserve my efforts and any student who is disruptive or argumentative should be dealt with swiftly, openly, and with no sympathy. (Good students *do* deserve our efforts, but we also need to put out some effort to see that the less-than-good students also have a chance to *become* good students. This may mean a discussion with them privately to see what we might be able to do to make things more interesting to them.)

I DO: I DON'T:
( )   ( )   12. I feel that the teacher is the most important person in the classroom, since the students would be helpless without the teacher. (There is a little "chicken-and-egg" problem with this philosophy. Try to imagine a classroom without a single student, and the instructor up teaching away. There is not much learning going on without the students. There is a possibility that learning can take place without a teacher—with self-directive material—but little chance of it taking place without students.)

I DO: I DON'T:
( )   ( )   13. I believe that a good, enthusiastic, well-illustrated lecture will get the desired results as far as learning is concerned. (The absence of the good, enthusiastic, well-illustrated lecture certainly will leave the job undone, but there has to be one other element: *the students need a reason for learning.* A good presentation is important, but it can't carry the whole load. The students need some motivation other than the excitement of the teacher. They need some internal motivation for the results to be completely satisfactory.)

I DO: I DON'T:
( )   ( )   14. I think an experienced teacher can tell by looking at students whether or not they are getting the information. Inexperienced instructors need feedback because they haven't developed this

skill. (There is an abundance of information to show that about the only thing we can tell for certain from looking at students is that when one is leaning back on his or her neck, mouth open, eyes closed, with resonant sounds coming forth from the mouth, not much learning is taking place. Beyond that, a nod or a bright eye doesn't tell us much about what is going on inside the mind.)

I DO: I DON'T:
( )   ( )   15. I feel that teachers who spend too much time getting feedback are insecure and don't trust their teaching skills. (Studies indicate the opposite may be true: teachers who don't allow the students to comment or give feedback may doubt their ability to get information across and can't face that reality; so they do all the talking, preferring to assume that the students are getting it because it is being put out. There is no substitute for feedback, and the best feedback comes as information is being presented, not as a final test when it is too late to react to the feedback.)

I DO: I DON'T:
( )   ( )   16. I believe that teachers should be enthusiastic about the subject they are teaching, and avoid teaching those things they can't get excited about. (If we only are good at teaching those subjects we are enthusiastic about, then we aren't much use as a teacher. Our excitement in teaching should come over *producing learning*, not selling a subject. If we can't get excited over the prospects of students going away from a class knowing something about a subject or being able to do something as a result of being in our class, then we have missed the joy of teaching.)

I DO: I DON'T:
( )   ( )   17. I think the ideal situation in which to teach is where the students are lined up in rows in front of me, I'm behind a speaker's stand, and my

whole lecture is spread out before me on the stand. (Since this represents a majority of the lectures that are given, it would seem that we have found the ideal. We may have found the most comfortable and most secure position for the instructor rather than the ideal learning situation. Students lined up in "military" fashion, waiting for the leader to give the marching orders, with the teacher behind the symbol of authority—the speaker's stand—and all the notes spread out so it is impossible to relate to the students, isn't a picture of a good teacher-learner relationship. The teacher who is tied to a set of notes, frozen to the stand, and separated from the students isn't going to accomplish nearly as much as the teacher who can leave the security of the stand and notes, walk before the students, stroll to the board, stop and look at the students, answer questions without getting off the subject, and be relaxed doing it.)

Well, how did you do? If you are determined to fail at lecturing, you will have to make certain that you can honestly check "I DO" on every item. If you discovered that you checked "I DON'T" on a few of the items, then you have some work to do. It will be difficult, *but many before you have succeeded in failing,* so don't give up hope. On the other hand, if you are interested in *not* being a failure at lecturing, then you will have to honestly be able to answer each of these statements "I DON'T." Here, again, it is difficult, but many have been able to do it. *You can too*!

VIII.

APPENDIX B

SOME CHARACTERISTICS OF A GOOD TEACHER/LECTURER

The following list of good characteristics is nowhere close to exhaustive, but will provide a basis for self-examination. It primarily has to do with the teacher's use of the teacher/student relationship, especially with regard to the lecture as a teaching tool. Rate yourself and see how you come out. There is no "passing" score. You must set your own standard. If you aren't satisfied with how you are doing, come back to this list in six months and see if you have improved.

GOOD   POOR
5 4 3 2 1   **1. Enthusiasm.** (The enthusiasm here isn't aimed at an excited kind of presentation, where the instructor jumps around, has a lot of exuberance, and talks with a voice that generates excitement and motivates students to listen. The best enthusiasm occurs when the teacher gets excited about teaching students to do some things they couldn't do before they came to the teaching-learning exercise. The enthusiasm shows itself when students have met certain objectives, and disappointment shows when the teacher has failed to get the students where he or she wanted them to go.)

GOOD   POOR
5 4 3 2 1   **2. Organization.** (The key isn't to be so organized that everything is laid out in order and is logical to the very end. The idea of organization is a *mental* thing, where the teacher is always aware of what is known and what isn't known. When a student asks a question, the

99

instructor immediately knows if he or she actually has the answer; and, just as important, he or she is able to access this information without fumbling around for some period of time. Since this instructor also knows what *isn't* known, time is saved by a simple admission of this. Steps are then made to research the answer, and agreement is made as to who will do the research.)

GOOD   POOR
5   4   3   2   1

3. **Knowledge of the Subject.** (While it is pardonable to not know something the first time it is asked, it is unforgivable to not know it the second time it is asked! Knowledge of the subject includes knowing about related subjects as well, and includes a reasonable amount of study on these subjects. This broadening of our base makes even what we know about a given subject more meaningful. It certainly improves our ability as a lecturer, especially when it comes to giving examples and answering related questions.)

GOOD   POOR
5   4   3   2   1

4. **Communications.** (This is much more than just ability to choose certain correct words and ways of expressing things. It is more than having a good vocabulary and a pleasing voice. Good communicating is built around several basic requirements. First, *know the message*. This is different from a "knowledge of the subject." The idea here is that the instructor never begins to lecture without first knowing just what is to be said. After the knowledge of the subject comes knowing how to put this message across. No good instructor would begin a lecture without first having decided on a set of opening remarks and what will be said to introduce the subject and maintain interest in that subject. Next comes *knowing the subject got there*. This is where feedback comes in, and good instructors never consider their communications effort com-

pletely finished until they have heard the students say or do the things being taught. Finally, there is the matter of *listening*. Of all the skills required by a good lecturer, this is the most important, and the most difficult to learn. Listening is more than just being silent while the students talk. It is a matter of listening for feedback, of comprehending what is said, and finding suspected weak points in the students' understanding of what has been taught.)

GOOD   POOR
5   4   3   2   1   **5. Student Relationships.** (For many years, the teacher was thought of as a molder of character more so than a facilitator of learning. Now we realize that the subject matter is most important, and the good teacher develops a relationship with the students based on their learning needs, rather than their social or psychological needs. There is an assumption that the students want to learn and that the true role of the instructor is to make this possible. When the students see the instructor in this role, then they are in a much better frame of mind to begin and carry on the learning activity.)

GOOD   POOR
5   4   3   2   1   **6. Teacher Role.** (There are two distinct roles in which teachers can see themselves. First, there is the *bearer of information*. There are three elements here: the information; the students who don't have this information; and the teacher who does have the information. It is the teacher's role to see that the students get that information; so the teacher stands between the students and the information. Second, there is the *facilitator of learning*. The same three elements exist, but in different ways. There are the students who don't have the information, the information itself, and the teacher who *directs the students to the infor-*

mation. The most successful instructors believe this last role fits the good teaching-learning environment.)

GOOD   POOR
5   4   3   2   1   7. **Platform Skills.** (The good teacher doesn't think of platform skills as the thing to carry an otherwise dull or boring subject. Rather, they are thought of as ways to enhance the presentation, maintain interest, and keep the students involved. Good teachers would classify *handling questions* as a more important skill on the platform than *good oratory*.)

MARTIN M. BROADWELL is co-founder of Resources for Education & Management, Inc., a firm specializing in management and supervisory programs and instructional design. He serves as consultant to business, industry, government, and education in the United States and abroad. He is the author of several books on supervision and training, including five published by Addison-Wesley Publishing Company: *The Supervisor as an Instructor: A Guide to Classroom Training; The Supervisor and On-the-Job Training; The New Supervisor; The Practice of Supervision: Making Experience Pay;* and *The New Hospital Supervisor.* He is also the author of two books published by CBI Publishing Company: *Moving Up to Supervision* and *Supervising Today.* Mr. Broadwell has written many articles published in the United States and abroad.